PEOPLES
of
EUROPE

Bosnia and Herzegovina

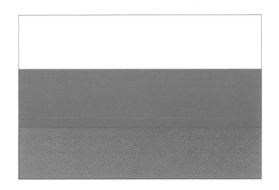

Bulgaria

Croatia

Cyprus

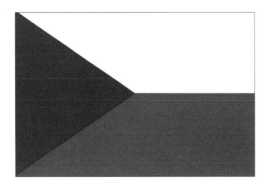

Czech Republic

PEOPLES
of
EUROPE

Volume 2
Bosnia and Herzegovina– Czech Republic

MARSHALL CAVENDISH
NEW YORK • LONDON • TORONTO • SYDNEY

Marshall Cavendish Corporation
99 White Plains Road
Tarrytown, New York 10591-9001

Website: www.marshallcavendish.com

Consulting Editor:
  Wendy Sacket, Coast Learning Systems, Coastline Community College

Consultants:
  Ian Barnes, Principal Lecturer in History and Politics, University of Derby
  Robert Hudson, Senior Lecturer in History and Politics, University of Derby
  Martyn Rady, Reader in Central European History, School of Slavonic and East European Studies, University College London

Contributing authors:
  Ian Barnes
  Neil Champion
  Robert Hudson
  Fiona Macdonald
  Clare Oliver
  Gillian Stacey
  Philip Steele

Discovery Books
  Managing Editor: Paul Humphrey
  Project Editor: Helen Dwyer
  Design Concept: Ian Winton
  Designer: Barry Dwyer
  Cartographer: Stefan Chabluk

Marshall Cavendish
  Editor: Marian Armstrong
  Editorial Director: Paul Bernabeo

The publishers would like to thank the following for their permission to reproduce photographs:
  AKG London (62, 76, 92, 93; J. Chaldej: 63; PK-Photo [Pebal-Speer]: 52); Sue Cunningham Photographic (67 bottom, 73, 90, 96 bottom, 99, 100); Hutchison Library (88 bottom; Melanie Friend: 64, 65, 66, 69, 70 top & bottom, 71, 72, 79; Juliet Highet: 56); Crispin Hughes: 54 bottom, 78, 80; Nigel Sitwell: 74, 81; Liba Taylor: 101, 103 top & bottom); Panos Pictures (Marc French: 77, 83; Heldur Netocny: 55, 59; Bill Stephenson: 54 top; Liba Taylor: 94, 95 top; Andrew Testa: 53; Gregory Wrona: 102); David Simson - DASPHOTOGB@aol.com - B-6940 SEPTON (cover, 84, 86, 87, 88 top, 89, 95 bottom, 97, 98); Still Pictures (Nigel Dickinson: 50, 57; Ron Giling: 60; Hartmut Schwarzbach: 68; Jecko Vassilev: 67 top, 96 top)

(cover) A young girl at a fiesta in Valencia, Spain.

Editor's note: Many systems of dating have been used by different cultures throughout history. *Peoples of Europe* uses B.C.E. (Before Common Era) and C.E. (Common Era) instead of B.C. (Before Christ) and A.D. (Anno Domini, "In the Year of the Lord").

In order to represent the diacritical marks used in various European languages, much of this reference work is printed in fonts created by Linguist's Software of Edmonds, Washington, www.linguistsoftware.com.

Library of Congress Cataloging-in-Publication Data

Peoples of Europe.
     p. cm.
   Includes bibliographical references and index.
   Contents: v. 1. Albania-Belgium -- v. 2. Bosnia-Herzegovina--Czech Republic -- v. 3.
Denmark-France -- v. 4. Germany-Hungary -- v. 5. Iceland-Liechtenstein -- v. 6.
Lithuania-Netherlands -- v. 7. Norway-Romania -- v. 8. Russia-Slovakia -- v. 9.
Slovenia-Switzerland -- v. 10. Ukraine-Yugoslavia.
   ISBN 0-7614-7378-5 (set) -- ISBN 0-7614-7379-3 (v. 1) -- ISBN 0-7614-7380-7 (v. 2)
-- ISBN 0-7614-7381-5 (v. 3) -- ISBN 0-7614-7382-3 (v. 4) -- ISBN 0-7614-7383-1 (v.
5) -- ISBN 0-7614-7384-X (v. 6) -- ISBN 0-7614-7385-8 (v. 7) -- ISBN 0-7614-7386-6
(v. 8) -- ISBN 0-7614-7387-4 (v. 9) -- ISBN 0-7614-7388-2 (v. 10) -- ISBN
0-7614-7389-0 (v. 11 : index vol.)
   1. Europe--Civilization--Encyclopedias. 2. Europe--History--Encyclopedias. 3.
Europe--Description and travel--Encyclopedias.

D9 .P45 2002
940'.03--dc21
                                                                        2002019490

   ISBN 0-7614-7378-5 (set)
   ISBN 0-7614-7380-7 (v. 2)

Printed and bound in Hong Kong
07   06   05   04   03   02   6   5   4   3   2   1

Contents

BOSNIA AND HERZEGOVINA

BOSNIA AND HERZEGOVINA (USUALLY SHORTENED TO BOSNIA) IS A MOUNTAINOUS COUNTRY IN SOUTHERN EUROPE.

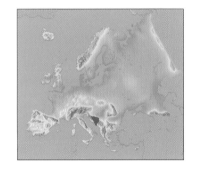

Almost all of Bosnia is mountainous, and nearly half the land is covered with thick forests of beech, oak, fir, and pine. River valleys between the mountains are fertile and suitable for growing crops and grazing cattle. The only low-lying area is in the east.

The Sava River forms much of the northern border with Croatia. Two other important rivers, the Neretva and the Drina, flow through the south, while the Bosna River lies in the north. A short coastline borders the Adriatic Sea.

CLIMATE

Northern Bosnia has hot summers and cold winters. Heavy rains fall as snow in the mountains, where winters are long and very harsh. Conditions in southern Bosnia are milder and drier, with typically Mediterranean weather.

Sarajevo

Average January temperature:	*30°F (-1°C)*
Average July temperature:	*66°F (19°C)*
Average annual precipitation:	*36 in. (91 cm)*

A Bosnian mother and her daughter outside their farmhouse in a fertile valley. Most farms are small and are owned and worked by families.

A Divided Land

The earliest traces of settlement in Bosnia (BAHZ-nee-uh) date from around 4500 B.C.E. Bosnia's people were conquered and ruled by the Romans during the first century C.E. Soon after 600 the region was invaded by Slav (SLAHV) peoples from the east. By the 800s two powerful Slav kingdoms, Croatia (kroe-AE-shuh) and Serbia (SUHR-bee-uh), dominated the region.

These Slavs occupied a frontier where two branches of the Christian church met. To the west, where most Croats (KROE-ats) lived, the Roman Catholic Church was powerful. To the east, the home to many Serbs, the Eastern Orthodox Church was in control.

For hundreds of years modern-day Bosnia was fought over by Croatia, Serbia, and Hungary. Bosnia became an independent state briefly from 1376 to 1391. From the 1300s onward, Bosnian, Serb, and Croat lands were attacked by armies of the Ottoman rulers of Turkey. Most of Bosnia was conquered by 1463. The southern region, the duchy of Herzegovina (HERT-seh-gaw-vee-nah), had fallen to the Turks by 1482. The Ottoman Turks introduced the faith of Islam to Bosnia. Over the years Islam became Bosnia's most widespread religious faith.

Turkish power weakened in the nineteenth century, and after the neighboring state of Serbia won freedom from Ottoman rule in 1829, many people in Bosnia also began to demand independence. The country became so unstable that, in

1878, the adjoining and powerful Austro-Hungarian Empire claimed Bosnia for itself, and in 1908 it officially annexed Bosnia. Revolutionary movements demanded independence. In 1914 a Bosnian Serb shot Archduke Ferdinand, the heir to the Austro-Hungarian throne, who was visiting

FACTS AND FIGURES

Official name: *Bosna i Hercegovina*

Status: *Independent state*

Capital: *Sarajevo*

Major towns: *Banja Luka, Zenica, Mostar, Tuzla, Bihać*

Area: *19,741 square miles (51,129 square kilometers)*

Population: *Between 3,800,000 and 4,400,000 (The precise figure is hard to ascertain because of many refugees and wartime genocide.)*

Population density: *192–223 per square mile (74–86 per square kilometer)*

Peoples: *44 percent Bosnians; 31 percent Serbs; 17 percent Croats; 8 percent other, including Roma, Jews, and Hungarians*

Official languages: *Three dialects of Serbo-Croat (Bosnian, Serbian, Croatian)*

Currency: *Convertible mark*

National day: *Independence Referendum Day (March 1)*

Country's name: *The medieval kingdom of Bosnia took its name from the Bosna River around which it was based. The meaning of* Bosna *is unknown.* Herzegovina *means "duke's land," and it refers to the medieval duchy of that name.*

Time line:	Bosnia part of Roman empire	Slavs arrive	Region divided between kingdoms of Serbia and Croatia	Independent Bosnia	Ottoman Turks rule the region; many Bosnians become Muslim
	1st century c.e.	600s	800s	1376–1391	1463–1878

The commander of the pro-German Bosnian Army inspects an antitank gun in 1941. Other Bosnians fought against the German invaders.

Sarajevo (sar-uh-YAE-voe). This sparked off an international political crisis, which eventually led to World War I (1914–1918).

After the war the Austro-Hungarian Empire ceased to exist. Bosnia became part of a new independent state, the Kingdom of the Serbs, Croats, and Slovenes. This was named Yugoslavia ("South-Slav" in Serbo-Croat) in 1929. The new country contained too many different peoples and cultures to work well together. Life in Bosnia became even more difficult after the outbreak of World War II (1939–1945). In 1941 German Nazi troops invaded. For the next four years, Bosnia was ruled by Germany's ally, Croatia. Throughout Yugoslavia fierce resistence against the Germans, the Croats, and their allies was led by a Croat guerrilla commander, Josip Broz Tito.

At the end of the war Yugoslavia was free from German rule. At first Tito (at this point head of the Yugoslav Communist Party) planned a government like that of the communist Soviet Union (see RUSSIA), but in 1948 he quarreled with Soviet leader Joseph Stalin and introduced his own fairly moderate style of communist rule. Each region of the country was allowed to keep its separate identity and to manage some of its own domestic affairs.

Tito aimed to turn Yugoslavia into a modern industrial state, building many factories and mines, especially in Bosnia. He also tried to keep all the different peoples of Yugoslavia living and working peacefully together.

After Tito's death in 1980, a new Collective State Presidency was set up, with members from each region. In 1989 the new Presidency introduced multiparty democracy, but Slovenia and Croatia began to seek independence. Serbs were spread across all regions of Yugoslavia, and they wanted Serbia to rule the large area, including Bosnia, that the medieval kingdom of Serbia had once controlled. In 1991 Bosnia, Slovenia, and Croatia broke away from Yugoslavia, declaring themselves independent.

In 1992 Bosnian leaders held a referendum to give people in Bosnia the chance to approve or disapprove the country's new independent status. Serbs living in Bosnia, supported by Serbs in Serbia, reacted by staging violent protests. Groups of Serb local militias and former soldiers from Tito's old Yugoslav People's

Bosnia becomes a colony of Austro-Hungarian Empire	Austro-Hungarian heir assassinated in Sarajevo; World War I follows	Bosnia becomes part of Kingdom of the Serbs, Croats, and Slovenes (later Yugoslavia)	Germans invade; Croatia controls Bosnia; guerrilla opposition led by Josip Broz Tito
1878	**1914**	**1918**	**1941–1945**

Army began a brutal campaign of "ethnic cleansing," an attempt to create ethnic purity by driving non-Serb people from their homes in Bosnia. At the same time Croats evicted Serbs from their homes in Herzegovina. By the end of 1992, around 70 percent of Bosnia was under Serb control, and the capital city, Sarajevo, was surrounded and besieged by Serb forces.

The United Nations imposed sanctions on Bosnia and sent a peacekeeping force to deliver humanitarian supplies to the many thousands of refugees who had fled from their homes. But the fighting—and the killing—continued. Atrocities were committed by soldiers and militias on all sides. In the three years following 1992, over 250,000 people were killed in Bosnia, 200,000 were wounded, and 13,000 were permanently disabled. Thousands of men were tortured, and women and girls were sexually attacked. Women and children were traumatized from seeing husbands, fathers, brothers, and sons kidnapped or executed by militia gangs. Even today, farmers, travelers, and children playing are killed or injured by exploding shells and land mines.

In 1994 Muslims and Croats in Bosnia agreed to form a new nation, but the Serbs continued fighting. In 1995 attacks by United Nations' forces on Serbs surrounding Sarajevo, plus high-pressure diplomacy, led by the United States, forced Serbian, Muslim, and Croat leaders to agree to the Dayton Accord.

The Dayton Accord kept Bosnia's borders as they were in Tito's time and set up a new government for all of Bosnia. The new government is responsible for establishing foreign, economic, and financial policy. Within Bosnia, local government is now divided into two separate states: the Federation of Croat and Bosniac Entities in the center and west (where mostly Muslims and Croats live) and the Bosnian Serb Republic in the north and east (occupied almost entirely by Serbs). Each looks after local affairs in its own part of the country.

Since the 1990s war, political parties have increasingly attracted support along religious or ethnic lines. In local elections held in the autumn of 2000, voters chose candidates according to their group identity rather than for their political beliefs or social and economic policies.

Muslim women from Srebrenica (sruh-BRAE-nih-kah) look through Red Cross photos of dead men's belongings, hoping to trace missing relatives, in 2000.

Bosnia becomes part of communist Yugoslavia, led by Tito	Tito dies	Multiparty democracy introduced	Bosnia declares independence	Civil war; ethnic cleansing; Sarajevo beseiged by Serbs	Dayton Accord; new multi-ethnic, democratic government formed
1945	**1980**	**1989**	**1991**	**1992–1995**	**1995**

A Muslim grandfather and grandson in a refugee camp read their holy book, the Koran. In many Bosnian families the only males still alive are old men and boys.

(ROE-muh-nee), and marry and bring up their children within their own community.

Religion is still important in shaping each group's sense of its own identity. Often, however, this is a matter of culture and tradition, rather than deep personal faith. Most Bosnian Muslims still follow the faith of Islam. Unlike people in some other Islamic countries, Bosnian Muslims do not adhere strictly to all Islamic laws. For example, Muslim men and women mix freely in public and drink alcohol. Muslim women do not veil their faces. Many Serbs are still members of the Eastern Orthodox branch of the Christian Church, and many Croats are still Roman Catholic.

In spite of the importance of religious tradition in Bosnian politics, Bosnia is a

Religions, Dialects, and Cultures

The most recent Bosnian government figures show that about 44 percent of the population call themselves Bosnian Muslims, about 31 percent say they are Serbs, and about 17 percent identify themselves as Croats. There are also minority groups living in Bosnia, including Roma (ROE-muh), Jews, and Hungarians.

The ancestors of the Roma people came from India via Iran and Armenia, arriving in Europe in the 1300s. Today the Roma make a living from odd jobs such as mending metal and leather objects, weaving baskets, and making brushes. They speak their own language, Romani

Roma women sell new and secondhand goods in a Sarajevo street market. The Roma people are some of Bosnia's poorest citizens. They are often treated as social outcasts.

secular state, which allows no special power in government to religious leaders.

In everyday life, traditions of religious observance can sometimes keep people apart. Roman Catholic Croats and Orthodox Serbs celebrate important Christian festivals, such as Christmas and Easter, on different days. Muslims do not observe these days at all, but they have their own festivals whose dates change from year to year.

Each group speaks its own dialect of the national language, which is known as Serbo-Croat. The dialects are all closely related, but they use different words and phrases, reflecting each group's history and culture. Many Serbs use a Cyrillic (sih-RIHL-ihk) alphabet (like the letters used to write Russian). The Croats use a Latin alphabet (like the letters used in this book). For prayers and religious study, Bosnian Muslims use Arabic, the Islamic holy language, but they use Serbo-Croat, written in a Latin alphabet, for everything else.

For centuries Sarajevo and other big cities were proud of their tolerant,

multicultural communities, where members of different groups lived side by side. However, since the war of the 1990s, the different peoples of Bosnia have treated one another with understandable suspicion. In particular, feelings of bitterness and fear remain in towns and villages where citizens were killed by rival militia groups. Non-Serb refugees expelled

The Siege of Sarajevo

For almost three years, from 1992 to 1995, Sarajevo was under siege. Serb soldiers, stationed high on the mountains overlooking the city, bombarded its buildings with shells and terrorized its citizens with deadly sniper fire. It was dangerous to look out a window or to walk down a city street. The Serbs prevented food, water, medical supplies, and many other necessary items from entering the city. People were hungry, sick, and very cold. Shops had nothing to sell, and restaurants had no food to serve. It was too dangerous for pupils and teachers to go to school. Many Sarajevo citizens made heroic efforts to keep the city functioning as well as they could. Doctors, ambulance drivers and fire-fighters did all they could to save lives. Journalists and communications workers struggled to keep citizens in touch with one another and to send news of their sufferings to the outside world.

Grieving families tend war graves at Lion Cemetery on the outskirts of Sarajevo. Most of the citizens who died during the siege of Sarajevo are buried here.

from their homes in the Bosnian Serb Republic claim that local government officials who permitted, or even encouraged, ethnic cleansing by Serbs are still in power. For this reason they are too frightened to return home to rebuild their houses, businesses, and farms that were destroyed during the war.

Among educated city dwellers, marriage between people from different groups was, until recently, accepted without question. This pattern was disrupted by the war in the early 1990s and the mistrust that has followed. Mixed marriage is rare in country villages, which are often dominated by a single group.

Until recent years, marriages were arranged between families, but now young people decide who they want to wed. In the past many Bosnian people lived in extended families called *zadruga* (zuh-DROO-gah), with several generations sharing one home and working together. People often used networks of family connections to find work or to help in hard times. Today, most families are small, just parents and children.

Country and City Life

Over half of the Bosnian people still live and work in the countryside. Most country homes, both old and new, are small and simple but have access to clean water, good drainage, and electricity supplies. However, nearly two-thirds of Bosnia's houses were damaged during the war in the 1990s, and nearly one-fifth were totally destroyed.

After World War II over two million Bosnians left the countryside, seeking a better life in the towns and cities. Housing was built for them in the center of cities, usually subsidized apartments built by the government or state-run enterprises. Until the 1990s war, many cities, such as Sarajevo and Mostar (MOE-stahr), were famous for their beautiful architecture. There were graceful bridges, fine family houses built around courtyards, narrow lanes lined with traditional craft workshops, and splendid mosques and meeting halls. On warm

Ancient Ottoman-style buildings by the Neretva (NEHR-eht-vah) River in the city of Mostar. Much Ottoman architecture was destroyed in the 1990s war.

A farmer carries a load of hay home from his fields on a wooden cart pulled by two horses. Bosnian farmers have few modern machines to help them with their heavy work.

summer evenings citizens walked and talked in the streets, met friends in restaurants and cafés, or watched street entertainers. In winter they could go to the theater to enjoy plays or the latest movies. Sarajevo was famous as a cosmopolitan cultural center and was also a popular ski resort that played host to the 1984 Winter Olympic Games. Bosnian families and sports enthusiasts made weekend trips to the snow-covered mountains that towered above the city streets.

Since the war in Bosnia ended, the inhabitants of big cities like Sarajevo and Mostar have made great efforts to rebuild their cities by restoring some of their schools and vibrant centers of business, entertainment, and the arts. Hotels and restaurants are slowly re-opening, and new conference facilities for businesspeople are being constructed. Almost all shops, cafés, markets, and theaters are busy again, and Sarajevo's streetcars rattle through streets full of office workers and shoppers. In their leisure time, Bosnians are free once more to relax by going to concerts, watching soccer, and taking part in outdoor sports. To show its new confidence and its hopes for the future, the city of Sarajevo launched an official bid to host the Winter Olympics in 2010.

An Old-fashioned Economy

Bosnia is rich in natural resources. It has large deposits of coal, iron, bauxite, manganese, and copper and extensive forests that provide timber. Hydroelectric plants use power from mountain rivers to generate cheap electricity.

Before the recent war, the Bosnian economy relied on old-fashioned heavy industries, with factories making iron, steel, aluminum, textiles, clothing and footwear, chemicals, and electrical goods. During the war, production fell by 80 percent. Unemployment rose to high levels throughout Bosnia. Since 1995, Bosnia has received large amounts of international aid to help rebuild its economy. By the year 2000 the Bosnian economy was slowly recovering, although unemployment was still high and many businesses remained unprofitable.

Compared with large farm businesses in the United States and Europe, Bosnian farms are small and inefficient. Most farms are run by families who consume the farm produce and do not pay themselves wages. The chief crops are wheat, corn, fruit, and vegetables. Farmers also keep sheep, cows, and goats.

War-damaged Health and Education Services

Bosnia's well-developed health-care services were badly disrupted by the recent war. Hospitals and clinics were destroyed, and doctors and nurses were killed or injured. In many parts of the country, water and sewer systems have been damaged or destroyed. Even so, on average, a man in Bosnia can expect to live until he is about 69 years old, and a woman can expect to live until she is 74.

Most children stay in school until they are 16, and many continue their studies at a college or university. There are also colleges where working people can continue to study part-time. Education was, however, badly disrupted by the 1990s war.

Since 1995, international organizations and voluntary agencies have worked hard in Bosnia to provide food and shelter for refugees and to help rebuild shattered homes, hospitals, and schools.

Clothes of an Earlier Age

Until the mid–twentieth century, Bosnia was famous for its wide variety of clothes. These were made of handwoven wool or linen cloth and decorated with metallic thread, colorful embroidery, and silver coins. For a man, the clothes included breeches, a cummerbund (a wide sash worn round the waist), a full-sleeved shirt, a waistcoat, and a flowerpot-shaped hat called a fez. Women's clothes also featured a shirt and waistcoat or jacket, together with dimije *(dih-MEECH-yuh: long and baggy pants) and boots. Many women covered their hair with an embroidered kerchief or scarf. Today these clothes are hardly ever worn, and young Bosnian women, especially in cities, like to follow the latest fashion trends from Paris, London, New York, or Milan.*

Stuffed Vegetables and Spicy Sausages

Until recently, all Bosnian dishes were based on local meats and vegetables. These could be served fresh, but they were often dried, smoked, salted, or pickled to preserve them for winter use. Popular dishes included *cevapcici* (suh-VAPS-chee: kebabs), *pljeskavica* (plee-ehs-kuh-VEE-kuh: meat patties), *pita* (PEE-tuh: pastry filled with meat or vegetables), *lonac* (LOE-nahk: meat and vegetable stew), *dolma* (DOEL-muh: stuffed vegetables), fancy bread, sometimes sprinkled with nuts or poppy seeds, and sweet, sticky pastries. Smoked meats and sausages, often flavored with spices, were specialties of many country districts, together with local cheeses and spicy red peppers. Wild foods, such as berries and mushrooms, were gathered from the forests in autumn.

These traditional foods remain popular, especially in restaurants called *aschinicas* (AHSH-nih-kahz), but during the late twentieth century, many American-style fast-food restaurants opened in cities and towns. They serve internationally popular snacks such as pizza and burgers. Cafés serving cakes and pastries, fruit juice, strong black coffee, and hot chocolate are popular places for people to meet and exchange news and views. Apart from coffee, beer is the Bosnians' favorite drink. *Slivovtz* (SLIH-voe-vihtz), a plum brandy, and *loza* (LOE-zuh), a grape brandy, are popular with men, especially at celebrations.

Music for City and Country

Over the years, Bosnian music has been influenced by traditions and techniques from Europe and the Middle East. This has led to the development of several unique musical styles in different parts of the country. In towns and cities *sevdalinke* (zehr-duh-LIHN-kuh)—love songs—are most popular. They can be sung by men or women, and they are usually accompanied on the *saz* (SAHTZ), a long-necked string instrument with a gentle, plaintive sound. The tunes are haunting, with swooping scales and much ornamentation. The lyrics are always romantic and sad. One famous song contains the words "The Drina River flows downhill, its waters do not come from the rain or the snow, but from the tears of young girls." Folktales report how, in the past, some listeners were so grief stricken from hearing a tragic sevdalinka performed that they rushed out and shot themselves.

In the countryside of eastern Bosnia, a very different style of music is preferred. It is known as *izvorna* (ihr-VOOR-nuh), or roots music. Orginally performed at important festivals in the farming year, such as harvesttime festivals, it now

Bosnian girls playing in the shallows of the Bosna River in Sarajevo. After years of warfare, Bosnian families hope that their children will grow up to a peaceful future.

Beauty in the Home

For hundreds of years Bosnian art has been created to add pleasure to everyday living. To decorate Bosnian houses, craft workers carved beautiful wooden ceilings and screens and made elaborate iron gateways. Many rooms had built-in seats cushioned with handwoven textiles. Brightly patterned carpets and rugs covered the floors. It was the custom to present a newly married couple with a special handwoven rug that included their initials in the pattern. Women embroidered flowers and abstract patterns on silk to wear as part of their national costume or to furnish their homes.

features at many parties and dances held in villages on Saturday nights. It is usually perfomed by two vocalists singing in extremely close harmony and accompanied by fiddles and a *sargija* (SAHRZ-yuh), a louder, country-style version of a saz.

BULGARIA

BULGARIA LIES IN EASTERN EUROPE, with the Danube River as its border in the north and the Black Sea forming a natural barrier in the east.

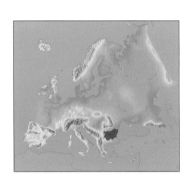

Bulgaria is a land of enormous physical contrasts, from the high mountains of the Balkan, Rhodope, Rila, and Pirin ranges to beautiful coastal plains along the Black Sea; from the lush Danube River valley in the north to the woods and plains of the interior. Mount Musala, at 9,596 feet (2,925 meters), is the country's highest peak.

CLIMATE

Bulgaria has hot, dry summers and cold winters. Winter snowfalls in the mountains can be very heavy. The mountains also receive most of the rain in the summer months. The plains around the Danube experience freezing weather and cold winds in the winter, but they are very hot in the summer. The coast around the Black Sea has the most moderate climate in the country.

Sofia

Average January temperature:	*28°F (-2°C)*
Average July temperature:	*70°F (21°C)*
Average annual precipitation:	*25 in. (64 cm)*

Women in the Dobrich (DAW-breech) region harvest grapes. These grapes will be used to make wine, a popular drink in Bulgaria and a valuable export.

The Bulgar Empire

People have lived in the region of Bulgaria (bul-GAR-ee-uh) for at least 6,500 years. By the 600s B.C.E. Greeks had established trading colonies along the Black Sea coast. Over the next few hundred years the region was conquered by a succession of powerful peoples, and in 46 C.E. it became a province of the Roman Empire.

The Roman Empire was finally broken up by invading peoples from central Asia.

One group of peoples, known as the Slavs (SLAHVZ), arrived in Bulgaria in the 500s. Some Slavs settled and became farmers. The modern Bulgarian language has evolved from the language of these Slavs.

The next invasion, in 679, was by the Bulgars (BOOL-guhrz), whose original homelands were to the east, between the Ural Mountains and the Volga River.

Soon the Slavs and Bulgars merged into one nation ruled by an emperor. Although it was called the Bulgar Empire, the Slavs were the more numerous, and by the tenth century they were the dominant ethnic group in the empire.

The Bulgar Empire became Christian in 865. Soon a national church developed, allied to the Eastern Orthodox family of Christian churches. At the same time, the empire expanded, capturing territory that included Macedonia.

From 1018 to 1185 the Byzantine (BIHZ-ehn-teen) Empire to the east ruled the Bulgar Empire. In the 1200s Bulgarian culture and military might dominated the region once again, and the borders of the empire were expanded.

FACTS AND FIGURES

Official name: *Republika Bŭlgariya (Republic of Bulgaria)*

Status: *Independent state*

Capital: *Sofia*

Major towns: *Plovdiv, Varna, Burgas, Ruse, Stara Zagora, Pleven*

Area: *42,823 square miles (110,912 square kilometers)*

Population: *8,200,000*

Population density: *191 per square mile (74 per square kilometer)*

Peoples: *85 percent Bulgarians; 8.5 percent Turks; 2.5 percent Roma; 2.5 percent Macedonians; 1.5 percent others, including Jews*

Official language: *Bulgarian*

Currency: *Lev*

National day: *Liberation Day (March 3)*

Country's name: *The name comes from the Bulgars, a people who settled in the region in the 600s C.E.*

Years of Ottoman Rule

Troops of the Ottoman Empire, based in Turkey, invaded Bulgaria in 1385. By 1389 most of the country was under Ottoman rule. Bulgarian nobles were crushed, and the church was controlled by the Sultan (ruler) of the Ottoman Empire. Some Bulgarians changed religion, from Christian to Muslim, to get good jobs within the new Ottoman political system.

Time line:	Romans conquer the region	First Slavic peoples arrive	Bulgars arrive	Bulgar Empire rules the region
	46 C.E.	500s	679	681–1018

Bulgarian culture managed to survive the hundreds of years of Ottoman rule. In isolated monasteries and in the smaller and remoter villages, especially in the mountainous regions, the local language, customs, and folklore and the Eastern Orthodox Christian religion were passed down through the generations.

In the 1700s, Bulgarian nationalism grew. People began to write books about Bulgarian history, and interest in its language, culture, and musical traditions was revived.

In the early 1800s, neighboring Serbia and Greece both rebelled against the Ottomans, and Bulgaria gave them support. The event that finally brought freedom to Bulgaria was a war between Russia and Ottoman Turkey. With Russian help, the Bulgarians recaptured their liberty in 1878. However, many Bulgarians lived outside the new country's borders, in places such as Macedonia, still under Ottoman rule. Some left these lands to join their fellow Bulgarians.

Bulgaria developed a political system with a king and a democratically elected parliament. The country's new rulers began the process of industrialization. Between 1878 and 1887, many large factories were opened to boost the economy of this mostly agricultural country.

Conflict Over Macedonia

Macedonia remained in Ottoman hands, much to the anger of Bulgaria, Serbia, and Greece. In 1912 they joined forces and declared war on Turkey. They were victorious, but they could not decide how best to divide up Macedonia among themselves. The following year Bulgaria declared war on its former allies but was defeated. Macedonia was divided between Greece and Serbia.

In World War I (1914–1918) Bulgaria sided with Germany and Austria against Serbia and Russia, seeing the chance to regain Macedonia if Serbia was defeated. Once again Bulgaria was on the losing side. This pattern

The Turkish-Russian War of 1878 brought the Bulgarians freedom from Turkish rule. Here the Czar of Russia, Alexander II (seated), surveys his army, which is besieging the Turkish-held town of Pleven (PLEH-vehn).

Bulgar Empire becomes Christian	Bulgar Empire is part of Byzantine Empire	Second Bulgar Empire emerges	Ottoman Empire takes over Bulgaria; introduces Islam	Bulgaria liberated from Ottoman Empire
865	**1018–1185**	**1200s**	**1389**	**1878**

Opponents of the Bulgarian government in the town of Lovech (loe-VEHCH) greet the Red Army in 1944. The Soviet invasion brought down the pro-German government.

repeated itself in World War II (1939–1945). The Bulgarian government sided with the Germans, with the hope of getting back Macedonia. However, unlike many other countries, Bulgaria did not give up its Jewish population to the German extermination camps.

A Communist State

Troops from the communist Soviet Union entered Bulgaria at the end of World War II and heavily influenced the direction that Bulgaria took. In 1946 Bulgaria became a republic, and in 1947 it declared itself a communist state. Under this regime, industrialization was given special importance. A strong central government owned the land and the industries. The government also controlled the lives of the people, crushing any private enterprise. The freedom of the church was taken away and many opponents of the government were imprisoned.

In 1954 Todor Zhivkov became leader of Bulgaria. He was to remain in power until 1989. In his long period of rule, he gave the Bulgarian people slightly more freedom. For instance, he allowed them their own private plots of land on which to grow food in their spare time.

Bulgaria, Greece, and Serbia go to war against Turkey	Bulgaria goes to war against its former allies, Greece and Serbia, over Macedonia	World War I; Bulgaria sides with Germany and Austria	World War II; Bulgaria sides with Germany
1912	**1913**	**1914–1918**	**1939–1945**

The Era of Change

In 1989 the Soviet Union lost control of the countries of eastern Europe (see RUSSIA). In 1990 a general strike brought down the Bulgarian Communist Party. This was followed by the first free elections since World War II. However, freedom has brought with it problems for the country. Bulgaria has suffered from successive weak governments. Corruption and crime have risen massively. Many people are without jobs, something almost unheard of under communist rule. Many Bulgarians still feel that Macedonia should be united with Bulgaria, and relations with Turkey are still strained. Bulgaria is looking to wealthy western Europe for inspiration and help and hopes one day to become a member of the European Union. But the road ahead for the nation is going to be a difficult one.

Peoples and Faiths

Bulgaria draws much of its rich culture and ethnic mix from four great empires of the past: Greek, Roman, Byzantine, and Ottoman. Mosques (Muslim places of worship) stand alongside churches and monasteries, and Greek and Roman remains intermingle with stark communist buildings of the mid–twentieth century. About 85 percent of Bulgaria's people are ethnic Bulgarians. There is also a large population of Turks, and smaller populations of Roma (ROE-muh), Macedonians, and Jews.

The Bulgarian language is spoken by nearly every Bulgarian today. It is closely related to the language spoken in neighboring Macedonia. Bulgarian uses the Cyrillic (sih-RIHL-ihk) alphabet that is used in Russia, Serbia, and Macedonia (see MACEDONIA).

Most people in Bulgaria are members of the Bulgarian Orthodox Church, a branch of Eastern Orthodox Christianity. Religion was suppressed under communism, but Orthodox Christianity always managed to survive. Today there are about 3,700 churches and more than one hundred monasteries

Muslims in the town of Khaskovo (KAHS-koe-voe) celebrate the opening of their restored mosque in 1995. Post-communist Bulgaria is becoming more tolerant of its Muslim communities.

Soviet Union invades Bulgaria	Bulgarian Communist Party takes power	Todor Zhivkov head of government	General strike brings down Bulgarian Communist Party; Bulgaria becomes multiparty democracy
1944	**1946**	**1954–1989**	**1990**

The Macedonian Question

When in 1878 Bulgaria became free of Ottoman rule, its ally Russia had promised it parts of Macedonia and northern Greece. Russia wanted to create a loyal "Greater Bulgaria." However, other European countries were worried that Russia would have too much influence in the region and changed the plan. Bulgaria did not get the land it was promised. Bulgarians say that most of the people in Macedonia speak a type of Bulgarian and therefore they have a right to the land. The question as to who should rule in this area has become even more difficult to answer since the creation of the Republic of Macedonia in the early 1990s (see MACEDONIA). Bulgaria officially recognizes this new country, but it refuses to recognize the Macedonians as a people different than themselves.

occupation. Few people practice Judaism, Roman Catholicism, and Protestantism.

In the twentieth century, Turks in Bulgaria suffered from extreme Bulgarian nationalism. Between 1912 and 1950 about half a million Turks left Bulgaria. In the 1980s the Bulgarian government attempted to force the remaining Turkish population to become more Bulgarian. They were no longer allowed to perform some religious ceremonies or have separate cemeteries for their dead. Mosques were closed, and wearing Turkish clothes and speaking the Turkish language were forbidden in public. Many Turks immigrated to Turkey in 1988 and 1989. It was only after the fall of the communist leader Zhivkov in 1989 that life improved for Bulgaria's Turkish citizens. Today there are around 700,000 Turks, mainly living in the northeast of the country and in the Rhodope (RAH-duh-pae) Mountains.

The Bulgarian Muslims are called Pomaks (POE-maks). Originally they lived in mountain villages in the south and southwest of Bulgaria, regions closer to the border with Turkey itself, the heart of the

scattered across the country. A lot of church land taken by the communists was given back by the government in 1990.

The other main religion in Bulgaria is Islam. Most of the Turks who remain in Bulgaria and most Roma are Muslims. So too are the Bulgarians who took up Islam under the Ottoman

The tobacco industry is important to the economy of Bulgaria. This Pomak (Muslim Bulgarian) family is sorting through the tobacco leaves, preparing them for the drying process.

Ottoman Empire. They remained separate from the Turks, retaining their Bulgarian customs.

The Bulgarian government started a campaign to absorb the Pomaks into mainstream Bulgarian culture in 1972. In 1989 Pomaks were refused passports to go to Turkey, where they felt they might be more welcome. Some were forced to change their Turkish Muslim birth names to Bulgarian ones. There were riots and strikes over these attacks on their rights. Today the situation is much calmer, and Bulgarians are once again more tolerant of different religions and choices.

There have been Roma in Bulgaria since at least the fifteenth century. They came originally

A Roma wedding is celebrated in the city of Plovdiv (PLAWV-dihf). The Roma live in tightly bonded family groups, and a wedding is a very important occasion for their community.

from India to Europe. They had no country to call their own, and so they were wanderers, sometimes welcomed or tolerated but often persecuted. Despite Bulgarian government attempts to bring an end to their traveling lifestyle, the Roma have been reluctant to settle in one place. The Roma have their own language, called Romani (ROE-muh-nee), and they form close-knit family groups. Most Roma children receive little schooling, and the Roma usually end up with the worst paid, least skilled jobs, such as laboring and street cleaning.

A Changing Economy, a Polluted Environment

Bulgaria has always been a mainly agricultural country, producing grains, soft fruits (such as cherries and strawberries), cotton, and tobacco. Today Bulgaria also

Nationalist Literature

Many of Bulgaria's great writers chose the struggles of their people for freedom and the injustices of harsh rulers as themes for their poems and novels. Ivan Vazov (1850–1921) wrote a novel, Under the Yoke, *about unsuccessful uprisings that took place in 1876 against the Ottomans. Vazov was deeply passionate about the history of his country and was involved with the nationalist movement in the second half of the nineteenth century. The poet Hristo Botev (1848–1876) was killed in the 1876 battles against the Ottomans. His poems are full of people who rebel against the domination of the Turks. In his poems Robin Hood-like figures nobly steal from the rich lords to give to the poor Bulgarian people.*

These men work in a brick factory. The soot and fumes produced in the brick-making process damage the workers' lungs and also contribute to Bulgaria's already serious air pollution.

has a thriving wine-producing industry, which accounts for around one-fifth of all agricultural produce sold abroad.

Bulgaria has some reserves of coal, oil, and natural gas, but two-thirds of its energy needs are supplied by other countries. There are also nuclear power plants and hydroelectric facilities. There are iron and steel industries, chemical plants, and textile mills. For most of its recent history, Bulgaria has traded mainly with other communist countries in the area, especially with the Soviet Union. Prices since the fall of communism have risen dramatically, and many people are worse off. The country has many skilled workers, but they are not used to working in a capitalist economy.

The rapid growth of industry under the communist governments has scarred the environment. In the rush to industrialize, little attention was paid to safety or protecting the landscape. Shortly after the fall of the Communist Party, it was estimated that about 60 percent of agricultural land was polluted by artificial fertilizers and pesticides. More than two-thirds of the rivers have been polluted, with one, the Yantra (YAHN-trah) River, being declared the dirtiest in Europe. The Black Sea coast is also heavily polluted, mostly from chemical plants. In the 1990s the government looked for help from abroad to solve its acute environmental problems.

At work in the offices of the Stock Exchange in Sofia. Plans to restructure the economy include encouraging private enterprise. Bulgaria also hopes to export more to the European Union.

Families shop for food in a Sofia supermarket. Today, if they have the money, Bulgarians can buy a greater variety of goods than was possible under the communist government.

exceeded the supply. Many newly married couples live with their parents because they cannot find a place to live for themselves.

When communism collapsed, rents and prices rose. The new market led to many people becoming homeless. In Sofia (soe-FEE-ah) the new homeless built a "tent city" to draw the government's attention to the problem.

In the countryside, homes are easier to find, and village houses, though older, are larger and more solidly built.

Unhealthy Lifestyles

Bulgarians have a high incidence of heart and respiratory (breathing) problems, caused in part by a diet rich in sugar and animal fat, abuse of alcohol and tobacco, and exposure to air pollution.

Crowded Housing

For the communist governments from the 1940s to the 1980s, housing was a priority. Many cheap apartment buildings were built in the towns to cater to growing urban populations. These are still the most available forms of accommodation for the average Bulgarian citizen. They are mostly cramped three-room apartments. Many families have to use the living room as a bedroom, and some even share kitchens with other families. Often several generations of the same family share a house or an apartment. Since the 1970s, the demand for urban housing has

Seasonal Celebrations

Many rituals preserve deep feelings about the people's relationship with the land and belief in its renewal. On February 14, at the festival of Trifon Zarezan (TREE-fawn zuh-RAE-zuhn), vines are sprinkled with wine to encourage good growth of the grapes and a full harvest in the autumn. Another popular custom, on the first day of March, is to give red-and-white threads to friends to wear.

Well into the twentieth century, traditional forms of medicine (using herbs, prayers, and special water said to have healing powers) were used by the people in the countryside. Governments have slowly built up hospitals and other medical resources since the 1940s, but Bulgaria is a long way behind current American and western European standards. The average life expectancy has reached 74 years for females and 67 for males.

In the 1990s, Bulgaria made a strong effort to develop its health-care system (with money from Western countries) by improving hospitals, employing more doctors and nurses, and educating people about healthy lifestyles. In 1991 the National Health Council was set up to produce an efficient, modern health system.

Rich Foods and Strong Drinks

Bulgarian food has been heavily influenced by the Ottomans. Dishes such as kabob (meat on a rod), *sarmi* (SAHR-mee: stuffed vine or cabbage leaves), and *kebapche* (keh-BAH-chuh: grilled meat rolls) are very similar to those found in Turkey or Greece. A favorite vegetarian dish is *sirene po shopksi* (sih-REHN-poe SHUP-skee), which is made with cheese, eggs, and tomatoes

Early in the morning a woman picks rose petals in the Valley of the Roses. Bulgaria is famous for its rose oil, used in perfumes, jams, and Turkish delight.

The Valley of the Roses

Forty miles north of Plovdiv, in the foothills of the Sredna (zuh-REHD-nuh) Mountains, is the Valley of the Roses. This area is reserved for growing thousands of roses. The land is heavily cultivated, with row upon row of the flowers stretching for miles. Roses have been grown here for their oil since the 1830s.

In May and early June of each year, the petals are picked at dawn before the hot sun can beat down upon them and burn off some of the precious rose oil. It takes up to six tons of petals to make two pints (one liter) of rose oil. The oil is used in making perfume, special jams, and expensive candies, such as Turkish delight (a jellylike confection, dusted with sugar). Weight for weight, rose oil is worth more than gold. Bulgaria supplies more rose oil than any other country in the world.

This couple is pickling vegetables in their kitchen. The Bulgarian taste for strong food with lots of flavor is partly a result of hundreds of years of Turkish influence.

and baked in an oven. These traditional dishes can be bought in little restaurants and cafés called *mehanas* (mu-HAE-nuz), which often have live music.

Bulgarian wine making goes back almost three thousand years. Today much Bulgarian wine is exported, but there is plenty left for the Bulgarians themselves to drink, both at home and in restaurants. Other alcoholic beverages include *slivova* (slih-VOE-vuh), or *rakiya* (RAHK-yuh), a type of plum brandy. Many Bulgarians love strong coffee, a taste passed down from the Turks. They usually drink it sweet and black.

New Directions in Education

Bulgaria has had free elementary schools since 1878. Today, school is compulsory for all children between the ages of 7 and 16. Bulgaria's high school system is one of the best in eastern Europe. Literacy is high, though the educational results of Roma children fall far below the national standards. The educational system, like almost everything else in Bulgaria, has undergone big changes. Russian was the second language of most Bulgarians for many years, but today young Bulgarians are more likely to be learning English, German, and French. Knowledge of these

This table on a Sofia street is well stocked with books. Today Bulgarians have access to a wide variety of literature and information and are able to express their political opinions freely.

widely used languages is considered essential for students if they are to find well-paying careers. After high school about three students in ten continue their education in institutions of higher learning, such as the University of Sofia.

Freedom of Expression

Ever since the early 1990s, the media in Bulgaria has had the freedom to discuss topics that would have been impossible under the communist government. Bulgarian reporters can now exchange news and ideas with reporters from other countries.

In 1987 there were only seventeen newspapers across the country, and most of these were local ones. By the early 1990s there were dozens of both national and local newspapers that reflected all types of political opinion. One national weekly paper, the *Sofia News*, was first published in the early 1990s and was instantly printed in ten different languages and sold throughout the world. Today the *Sofia Echo* is the leading English-language newspaper.

Musical Riches

Bulgaria has one of the richest musical traditions in Eastern Europe. Greek, Byzantine, Eastern Orthodox Christian, Ottoman, Roma, and Slav traditions have all added their particular flavor to the mix. Today the music is of two basic types: church music and folk music.

Bulgarian sacred music has its roots in the Eastern Orthodox church of Byzantium, dating back to at least the 800s. It can be heard in the churches of the towns and cities of Bulgaria, where people will gather together to sing the religious chants.

These boys are enjoying a music lesson at their school in a poor district of Plovdiv. The Bulgarian government is trying to improve educational standards across the country.

Folk music has its roots in the Bulgarian countryside. For hundreds of years country people have come together to celebrate a festival, a season, or a wedding with music and dance. The music is very distinctive, with a great variety of rhythms and speeds. It generally has a very complex melody.

There are regional differences as well. The folk music of the north and west is fast and abrupt, while that of the southeast is more melodic and flowing. Both men and women dance. Traditionally, women do not play instruments, but they do most of the singing.

Bulgarian folk instruments produce hauntingly memorable sounds. The most popular instruments are the *kaval* (kuh-VAHL), a long wooden flute; the *gadulka* (guh-DOOL-kuh), a small three- or four-stringed violin; the *gayda* (GIE-duh), a type of bagpipe made out of a goatskin; and the *tapan* (TUH-pahn), a large drum beaten with a stick. Other instruments include the *tambura* (tuhm-BOO-ruh), a long-necked,

A Unique Singing Style

Bulgarian women sing in a unique way. This singing style is often called open-throat singing, but in fact it is the opposite. The women sing with a constricted throat, forcing out a sound that is both strong and focused. They sing in harmony, in two or three parts, but the notes are often very close together and the harmonies sound harsh to Western ears. In the Pirin (PEER-ihn) Mountains some groups of women can sing two different two-part songs with different lyrics at the same time. Bulgarian women singers and choirs have been recorded extensively, and their CDs are popular around the world.

Many towns celebrate festivals with parades, folk music, and dancers in costume. This Festival of Roses at Kazanlŭk (kuh-zahn-LUHK) is a highlight of the summer.

four-stringed lute struck with a quill; the *dayre* (DIE-ruh), a tambourine; and the *zurna* (ZOOR-nuh), a kind of oboe. Today folk instruments are still played at village dances and weddings. Music for rural weddings is called *stambolovo* (stuhm-BLOE-voe). Stambolovo often involves six or seven different instruments in combination.

In the 1950s a movement was started to gather and record the songs and dances of the countryside. More than five hundred folk songs were adapted for the National Folk Ensemble by composer Philipp Kutev. This brought Bulgarian folk music an international reputation, which has grown over the years.

Mountain Sports

Bulgaria has a thriving and well-developed ski industry. It is based mostly in the mountains of the south

These teenage boys are enjoying a game of volleyball in a city park. Volleyball and soccer are popular sports among young Bulgarians in both urban and rural areas.

and west. Many Bulgarians go there between December and April to enjoy the downhill and cross-country skiing that is offered. The Vitosha (vih-TOE-shuh) Mountains, only 5 miles (8 kilometers) from the capital, Sofia, are very popular with the city's skiers.

Bulgarians also enjoy walking and climbing in mountain areas. The popular time for hiking is late spring and summer, although by midsummer it can become very hot in the lower mountains. Mountain shacks are provided as overnight accommodation for people on long hikes.

The most popular urban sport is soccer. Most children learn to play at school. Bulgaria's national team takes part in international competitions and has produced some world-class players.

Celebration for a Soldier

Eighteen-year-old Bulgarian men are required to serve in Bulgaria's armed forces. They spend eighteen months in the army or two years in the navy or air force. In the early 1990s about six thousand young men left the country illegally to avoid military service, and thousands more simply failed to turn up.

However, those who do leave for military service celebrate with a party before they go. If the recruit comes from a big town, his family will hire a band and reserve a restaurant. If he lives in a village, an outdoor street party is a more popular option. In both cases the guests eat, drink, and dance for many hours, and the recruit receives presents—usually money or shirts—from his friends and family.

CROATIA

CROATIA LIES IN SOUTHERN EUROPE, its long southwestern coastline bordering the Adriatic Sea.

In the east of the country is flat, fertile grassland, crossed by wide rivers—the Danube, the Drava, and the Sava. In the center rise barren, rocky mountains. In the north, there are low, rolling hills covered in forest. Along the coast, there are countless rocky inlets and over a thousand islands.

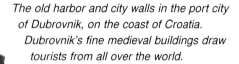

CLIMATE

Along the coast there is a mild Mediterranean climate, with short winters and long, dry summers. Inland the weather is much harsher, with hot summers and bitterly cold winters, especially on the eastern plains.

Zagreb

Average January temperature:	*32°F (0°C)*
Average July temperature:	*79°F (26°C)*
Average annual precipitation:	*34 in. (86 cm)*

The old harbor and city walls in the port city of Dubrovnik, on the coast of Croatia. Dubrovnik's fine medieval buildings draw tourists from all over the world.

A Slav Kingdom

The first traces of human settlement in the region of Croatia (kroe-AE-shuh) date between 4700 and 3900 B.C.E. From around 200 B.C.E. to the 400s C.E., the Romans ruled land along the coast and farther inland. The region was then divided between the Byzantine (BIHZ-ehn-teen) emperors, based in Constantinople (present-day Istanbul, in Turkey), and rival warlords.

During the 600s, the region was invaded by Slav (SLAHV) peoples, including Croats (KROE-ats), who arrived from farther north and east. By the 800s an independent Croat kingdom had formed and soon the people converted to Christianity. Then, around the year 1090, the Croatian king died, leaving no heirs, and the king of Hungary took over the throne.

This was the beginning of a struggle between Croatia and the rulers of Hungary that lasted for several centuries. It also involved Croatia in Hungary's many wars against the rich Italian city of Venice, which aimed to control the coast on both sides of the Adriatic Sea. In the midst of this fighting, the city of Dubrovnik (DOO-brawv-nihk) managed to stay independent, although Venice controlled the rest of Dalmatia (dal-MAE-shuh), the southern coastal region of Croatia, after 1420.

In the late 1300s the Ottoman Turks began to invade, and by 1526 much of Croatia was under Ottoman control. To prevent further Ottoman advance, the king of Hungary gave orders for the borderlands between his country and Ottoman territory to be specially fortified.

FACTS AND FIGURES

Official name: *Republika Hrvatska (Republic of Croatia)*

Status: *Independent state*

Capital: *Zagreb*

Major towns: *Split, Rijeka, Osijek, Zadar*

Area: *21,829 square miles (56,537 square kilometers)*

Population: *Between 4,300,000 and 4,800,000 (The precise figure is hard to ascertain because of many refugees and wartime genocide.)*

Population density: *197–220 per square mile (76–85 per square kilometer)*

Peoples: *78 percent Croats; 12 percent Serbs; 10 percent others, including Bosnians, Hungarians, Slovenes, Czechs, Albanians, Montenegrins, Roma, Italians, Slovaks, and Germans*

Official language: *Croatian*

Currency: *Kuna*

National days: *Statehood Day (May 30); Homeland Thanksgiving Day (August 5)*

Country's name: Croatia *is an anglicized form of the Croatian* Hrvatska. *The country is named after its main ethnic group, who call themselves* Hrvat. *In the Middle Ages, writers claimed it meant "people who occupy much territory."*

He invited volunteers to settle there and work as guards. These were mostly Serbs, fleeing from the Ottomans farther south and east. In this way, a stretch of Serb-occupied territory, called Krajina (krie-EE-

Time line:	First traces of human settlement along coast	Croats arrive from north and east	Croat kingdom formed	Croatia united with Hungary	Most of Croatia under Ottoman rule	Serbs settle Krajina
	4700–3900 B.C.E.	600s C.E.	800s	ca. 1090	1526	1550s

nah), was created in Croatia and Bosnia, far from other Serbian lands.

In 1699 the Turks were driven out of Croatia. In 1797, during the Napoleonic Wars, which caused upheaval throughout Europe, western Croatia was given to France. Then, after France was defeated in 1815, almost all of Croatia was ruled from Hungary, while Dalmatia was administered from Austria. Throughout the nineteenth and early twentieth centuries, there were increasing demands for Croatian independence.

A Failed Alliance

Austro-Hungarian power was seriously weakened during World War I (1914–1918). At the end of the war, Croatia became part of the Kingdom of the Serbs, Croats, and Slovenes (renamed Yugoslavia in 1929), along with Serbia, Bosnia, Macedonia, and Slovenia.

During World War II (1939–1945), Croatia was invaded by German Nazis and their Italian allies. Some Croats were sympathetic to Nazi aims. Many others joined the guerrilla opposition, led by Croatian communist Josip Broz Tito. At the end of the war, Yugoslavia

Armed members of the Croatian Ustaše (OOS-ta-shuh) movement in 1941. The Ustaše was an extreme nationalist organization that supported German invaders during World War II.

became a communist state. It was led by Tito and Croatia was administered as one of several federated regions. Each was allowed to keep its own independent identity, although policies that challenged Tito's moderate communism were banned. Within Yugoslavia, there was increasing tension between Croats and Serbs.

Tito remained in power until his death in 1980. He was succeeded by the Collective State Presidency. This arrangement satisfied no one, and throughout the 1980s there were demands for Croatian independence.

Conflict and Civil War

In 1989 the Yugoslav government introduced several political reforms that aimed to secure Serb domination in Yugoslavia. The next year, in the first multiparty elections since World War II,

Turks driven out of Croatia	Croatia ruled by Hungary and Austria	Croatia becomes part of Kingdom of the Serbs, Croats, and Slovenes (later Yugoslavia)	Yugoslavia becomes communist state	First multiparty elections; Franjo Tudjman elected president of Croatian region
1699	**1815**	**1918**	**1945**	**1990**

Franjo Tudjman, leader of the nationalist Croatian Democratic Union, was elected president of the Croatian region. In 1991 Tudjman declared independence for Croatia. Slovenia and Bosnia soon followed his example. However, Serbs living in Croatia did not agree with Tudjman's actions, and fighting broke out. The Croatian Serbs were supported by the government of Serbia. They encouraged the Serb-dominated Yugoslav Peoples' Army to occupy the areas of Croatia where Serbian people lived. The fighting was especially fierce around Vukovar (voo-KOE-vahr), in eastern Slavonia.

Families of soldiers and refugees who disappeared during the 1990s war light candles to remember them at a weekly memorial in Zagreb, the capital city of Croatia.

In 1992 Croatia was recognized as an independent country by the international community, and it became a member of the United Nations (UN). A UN peacekeeping force was sent to Croatia. A ceasefire was arranged with the Serbs, who withdrew from the Dubrovnik region but remained in control of other Croatian lands.

In 1993 fighting was renewed. Croats fought against Serbs not only in Croatia but also in neighboring Bosnia, where they hoped to take the heavily Croat region of Herzegovina (HERT-seh-gaw-vee-nah). There were bitter words and many atrocities on both Serbian and Croatian sides. Thousands of people were killed, and hundreds of thousands were forced from their homes as refugees.

In 1995 Croatian forces invaded Krajina and drove out almost all the Serbs (about 150,000 people), but it was not until 1998 that Serbian armies were persuaded to withdraw from Vukovar, the last territory they occupied in Croatia.

Since President Tudjman's death in 1999 and the defeat of his strongly nationalist Croatian Democratic Union party in elections early in 2000, Croatia has been governed by a coalition of center-left parties. They have promised to improve international relations, give greater freedom to the press, encourage economic development, and respect human rights.

Croatia declares independence; war between Croats and Serbs; Serbs driven out of Krajina	Serbs withdraw from last territory in Croatia	New coalition government promises social, economic, and political reforms
1991–1995	**1998**	**2000**

Croatia's Peoples

Croats form a large majority within Croatia. Some also live in neighboring countries. Many thousands of Croats left their country during the early years of the twentieth century. Today there are thriving Croatian communities in many parts of Europe (especially Germany) and in Australia, Canada, and the United States.

Serbs make up around 12 percent of the population. There are also many smaller ethnic groups who mostly originate from nearby lands such as Bosnia, Hungary, and Italy. Roma (ROE-muh) have lived in Croatia for many centuries, as have small communities of Jewish people.

A newly married Serbian couple and friends pose for photos during the 1990s war. Members of the wedding group carry the Serbian national flag, to show which side they support.

Pilgrimages

Many Roman Catholic Croats show their faith by taking part in pilgrimages (special journeys to holy places). There are many important places of pilgrimage in Croatia, including Sinj, where people believe that the Virgin Mary helped Croatians withstand an attack by the Ottoman Turks in 1715, and Karlovac (KAHR-luh-vahts), where a shrine is dedicated to Saint Joseph, the patron saint of Croatia.

Probably the most important shrine is at Marija Bistrica, where pilgrims come to visit a historic statue of the Virgin Mary carved from blackwood. Many Catholics believe that healing miracles have been performed at this shrine and that prayers said here have been answered. For over three hundred years, believers have made pilgrimages to see the Black Statue. Today over half a million pilgrims travel to Marija Bistrica every year.

Almost all of these people speak the official language, Croatian, as well as the mother tongue of their original homelands. Many Croatian people also speak German, especially if they work in the tourist trade.

For many Croats, religion is a sign of national identity. Until the twentieth century, they were allowed to use an ancient version of their native language (known as Glagolitic) instead of Latin for worship in Roman Catholic churches. Most Croatian Catholics still attend church services and take part in religious ceremonies on important festival days.

Many Hungarians and Italians living in Croatia are also Roman Catholic. Most Serbs are members of the Eastern Orthodox

Church; many Bosnians are Muslims; some Germans and Austrians are Protestants. There is also a small Jewish community, living mainly in Zagreb (ZAH-grehb).

Croatia today is a modern, democratic, secular state. The Roman Catholic church remains influential in public life, but it has no place in government.

A family strolls from church through the beautiful old streets of Dubrovnik. The tall bell tower of Dubrovnik's Roman Catholic cathedral is at the back of the photograph.

Daily Life in Croatia

The effects of the 1990s war along with rapid social change since the breakup of communist Yugoslavia are still being felt. Many people from minority groups, especially Serbs, lost their jobs in government-run offices and factories after the Croatian Democratic Union came to

Easter Celebrations

Throughout Croatia, Easter is celebrated with bonfires and beautifully decorated Easter eggs (often treasured as souvenirs). There are also shooting contests featuring antique pistols.

In Dubrovnik and on nearby islands, many ancient Easter customs survive. On Palm Sunday people bring bunches of spring flowers, cherry blossoms, palm leaves, and olive twigs decorated with flowers to church. These are blessed by priests, then taken home to hang in village houses for the next year as a powerful protection against bad luck. On Good Friday islanders walk to church in processions, accompanied by musicians playing sorrowful tunes.

power. During the fighting, thousands of people were killed, tens of thousands of homes were destroyed, and hundreds of thousands of people were forced to flee. Croatia also became home to refugees fleeing from the fighting in Bosnia. Around three-quarters of a million homeless people arrived in the country in 1992, mostly from Bosnia.

Within Croatia there are regional differences of lifestyle. Almost 60 percent of Croatia's population lives and works in towns. Urban society is sophisticated and cosmopolitan, especially along the coast. In towns, people live in concrete high-rise apartment buildings or in old stone houses.

Inland areas, especially Slavonia, are more rural. People living there earn their living from farming and forestry. The most important farm products are wheat, corn, sugar beets, sunflower seed, alfalfa, clover, olives, citrus fruits, grapes, vegetables,

Shoppers and streetcars on the streets of Zagreb. Zagreb is an industrial center, with factories producing electrical goods, cement, and pharmaceuticals.

beef, milk, butter, and cheese. Most village homes have clean water, drains, and electricity. Wherever they live, most Croatian families own cars, plus basic consumer goods, such as refrigerators and televisions.

Rebuilding the Economy

Croatia has valuable natural resources, including oil, coal, bauxite, and iron. There is some timber in the northern forests and fast mountain streams are used to generate electricity. These natural resources are used by factories making chemicals and plastics, machine tools, paper, textiles, and electronic goods. There are also petroleum refineries, iron and steelworks, shipyards, aluminum smelters, and timber mills. Most goods are made for local use, but some textiles, chemicals, and fuels are exported.

Let's Talk Croatian

Croatian is a version of Serbo-Croat, a Slav language also spoken by Bosnians and Serbs.

da *(DAH)*	*yes*
ne *(NEH)*	*no*
hvala *(HVA-la)*	*thank you*
nema na cemu *(NEH-ma na TSEH-moo)*	*you're welcome*
bog *(BOEG)*	*hello*
zbogom *(ZBOE-gehm)*	*goodbye*
oprostite *(oe-proe-STEET)*	*I am sorry*
sretno! *(SREHT-noe)*	*good luck!*

Island Traditions

In summertime, there are many festivals celebrated along the Croatian coast and on the islands. One of the most famous is the Sinjska Alka (SEEN-ska AL-kuh), a tournament, or mock battle, surviving from the Middle Ages. Participants, dressed in medieval costume and armor and mounted on horseback, take part in competitions designed to test "a steady hand and clear sight," such as catching a metal ring on the tip of a long lance.

Men from the island of Korčula, off the Dalmatian coast, perform the moreska dance. They carry weapons and wear costumes that are copies of medieval styles.

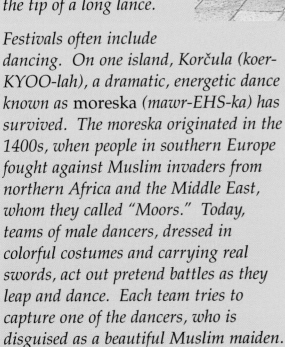

Festivals often include dancing. On one island, Korčula (koer-KYOO-lah), a dramatic, energetic dance known as moreska (mawr-EHS-ka) has survived. The moreska originated in the 1400s, when people in southern Europe fought against Muslim invaders from northern Africa and the Middle East, whom they called "Moors." Today, teams of male dancers, dressed in colorful costumes and carrying real swords, act out pretend battles as they leap and dance. Each team tries to capture one of the dancers, who is disguised as a beautiful Muslim maiden.

All businesses were badly damaged by the 1990s war. Roads, bridges, railroads, and power lines were destroyed, along with telecommunications links and water supplies. International travel and trade were almost impossible, and parts of the country were littered with land mines.

After the fighting ended in 1995, international organizations and voluntary agencies offered large amounts of aid to help rebuild the economy. About one-fifth of the workforce is without jobs. Many Croatian men leave their families to work overseas. Other current problems include dangerous air pollution, the destruction of trees caused by acid rain, coastal pollution, and overfishing.

However, there is good news for the economy, too. One of its most important sectors, tourism, is recovering quickly from the effects of the war. By 1999 the Croatian tourist industry employed over 200,000 people and generated about 12 percent of the national wealth. Tourist attractions include dramatic mountain scenery, a beautiful coastline and beaches, historic buildings, and vast national parks.

Health and Education

Croatian health care is good, but it was badly damaged by the recent war. Today there are still serious shortages of trained staff and medical supplies. In some places water and sewer systems were damaged or destroyed. Since 1995, international organizations and voluntary agencies have provided emergency aid, such as food, medical treatment, and shelter for refugees. They have also helped to rebuild schools and hospitals damaged by shells and bombs.

In spite of these difficulties, most Croatians still enjoy a good standard of health. On average, Croatian men live to be around 70 years old, and women live to be about 77. Child welfare is excellent, and most people choose to have small families.

Today, 97 percent of Croatians can read and write. Only about one in ten students go on to a university, although there are further education colleges where working people can study part-time.

Fresh Food, Preserved Food, Festival Food

Throughout the country, foods reflect local differences in climate, lifestyle, and natural resources. For example, *brodet* (BROE-deht), a fish stew with rice, is cooked in coastal regions, while *bobica* (BOE-bit-sa), a bean and sweet corn soup, is prepared in farming districts farther inland. Carp, eels, and even frogs are eaten as treats in riverside regions, and different local cheeses can be found throughout the country. In the south, where many fruit and nut trees grow, popular desserts include dried raisins and figs and cakes made with almonds and honey. In northern Croatia, where winters are long and harsh, many foods are preserved.

Juha od Krumpira

To make Juha od Krumpira (YOO-ha oed kroom-PIHR-a)—potato soup—you will need:

- *1 ¹/₂ lb (700 grams) potatoes*
- *2 oz (60 grams) butter or margarine*
- *2 oz (60 grams) smoked bacon*
- *1 medium onion*
- *1 tbsp (15 grams) paprika*
- *¹/₂ tsp (2.5 grams) dried oregano or marjoram*
- *1 tbsp (15 grams) flour*
- *salt and pepper (to taste)*
- *Approximately 35 fl oz (1 liter) vegetable stock (from a stock cube)*
- *8 fl oz (200 milliliters) plain yogurt*
- *2 cloves garlic, chopped*
- *small bunch of fresh parsley, chopped*

Wash and peel the potatoes and cut them into small cubes. Chop the bacon. Peel the onion and chop it finely.

Heat the butter or margarine in a large heavy pan. Add the bacon and onion and cook gently until the onion begins to soften. Add the potatoes, paprika, and oregano or marjoram, plus a little salt and pepper. Stir well, then sprinkle lightly with the flour. Stir again. Add the stock, mixing well. Cover the pan and boil gently until the potatoes are very soft.

When the potatoes are cooked, mash the contents of the pan very well or use a blender. Then return the soup to the pan. Stir in the yogurt, garlic, and parsley. Heat the soup very gently, stirring all the time, until it is almost boiling.

This quantity serves six people.

Meat is salted, smoked, or made into sausages flavored with garlic, spices, or wild herbs. Cabbages, beets, onions, and many other vegetables are pickled in salt or vinegar. Plums and berries are bottled or made into jam. Wild mushrooms, gathered from the woods, are carefully dried.

Foods with a foreign influence include Italian-style pasta, Turkish stuffed vegetables and pies, Hungarian paprika stews and sweet pastries, and light, elegant seafood dishes prepared in French style.

In big cities and along the coast, hotels and restaurants serve international food and fast-food snacks. However, local specialties are still popular, especially in the home. Favorites include stuffed sauerkraut rolls, called *sarma* (SAHR-muh), and *struckle* (STROO-kuhl), which are sweet curd-cheese pastries. Many dishes are linked to festivals: pork-and-potato stew is served on pilgrimages; codfish is eaten on Christmas Eve; and a hot-pepper sausage called *kulen* (KOO-lehn) is served at harvesttime.

Many different wines are produced in Croatia. Typically they are white and light in the north and red and full bodied in the south. In summer they are sometimes served mixed with water to make a cool, refreshing drink. There are also many different types of brandy made from grapes and plums.

A Thousand Years of Music

Croatia has a long, well-preserved musical tradition. Manuscripts containing religious music that was performed in churches have survived for over a thousand years. Many ancient Christmas carols, folk songs, and dances have also survived, including an energetic round dance called the *kolo* (KOE-loh). Folk tunes are played on the *tamburica* (tam-boo-REET-sa), a stringed instrument like a mandolin, or on violins. Along the coast, Italian-style serenades, played on guitars and accordions, are popular.

Sports in Croatia

The most popular sports are soccer and basketball. Croatia has one of the best soccer teams in the world. It reached the semifinals in the 1998 World Cup.

Croatian basketball players are also international stars. The most famous, Kresimir Cosic (1948–1995), was one of only three non-American players to have been elected to the world basketball Hall of Fame. Other very well known players include the late Drazen Petrovic, Toni Kukoc, and Dino Radja. The Croatian national basketball team has won medals at European and World Championships and was a silver medalist at the 1992 Olympic Games.

These swimmers and sunbathers are enjoying a card game on the shores of one of Croatia's inland lakes. Croatia's hot summers attract many tourists from northern Europe.

CYPRUS

CYPRUS IS A LARGE ISLAND in the
eastern Mediterranean Sea.

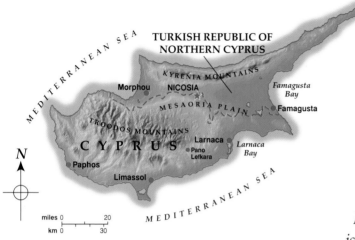

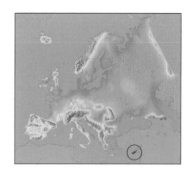

*Cyprus lies about 40 miles
(64 kilometers) south of Turkey in
the far east of the Mediterranean Sea.
Its jagged coastline shelters long sandy
beaches. In the north are the Kyrenia
Mountains. The central part of the
island is a flat plain, called the Mesaoria.
Farther south lie the Troodos Mountains.*

A black-clad woman from central Cyprus. Christian or
Muslim, most widows dress in black and wear headscarves
in mourning for their lost husbands.

CLIMATE

*Cyprus has hot, dry summers from mid-May to
mid-September and mild, rainy winters from
mid-November to mid-March. There is some
snowfall in winter, but only on high ground.*

Nicosia

Average January temperature:	*50°F (10°C)*
Average July temperature:	*82°F (28°C)*
Average annual precipitation:	*15 in. (38 cm)*

An Island Divided

Around 8,000 years ago people built
farming villages on Cyprus (SIE-pruhs).
These people started to work with copper
around 3500 B.C.E. About 4,000 years ago
Cyprus formed trade links with Anatolia
(Turkey), Syria, Egypt, and Crete and
imported pottery from the Greek kingdom

of Mycenae (mie-SEE-nee). When Mycenae was sacked in 1200 B.C.E., many of its inhabitants fled to Cyprus, dividing the island into ten city-states. Greeks became the largest ethnic group on Cyprus. Their language, religious beliefs, art styles, and even fashions remained dominant despite later settlements by others.

Over the next few centuries a succession of peoples—Assyrians, Egyptians, Persians, and Romans—conquered the island. In the first century C.E., the Cypriots (people of Cyprus) converted to Christianity. Cyprus became part of the Byzantine (BIZ-ehn-teen) Empire in 395 C.E.

Various invaders ruled the island over the centuries. England conquered Cyprus (1191) during the Christian Crusades against Islam, after which the island passed to Venice (1489), then to Ottoman Turkey (1571).

In 1878, after the Turks were defeated by the Russians, Turkey ceded Cyprus to the United Kingdom in exchange for protection against Russia. The British established a type of parliament but still taxed both Greek and Turkish Cypriots heavily. During the British occupation, many Turkish Cypriots immigrated to Turkey. The island became a useful supply and training base and naval station for British forces in both World War I (1914–1918) and World War II (1939–1945).

The Greek Cypriots called for *enosis* (EHN-oe-sees), or union, with Greece. This alarmed the Turkish Cypriots. In the 1930s resentment against the government grew. The United Kingdom reacted harshly to these protests, suspending the constitution,

censoring the press, and banning political parties. Nevertheless, 30,000 Cypriots served with British forces after the United Kingdom tried to defend Greece against the German army in 1941.

After 1945 the British refused to consider renewed calls for enosis. The Eastern Orthodox Church wanted to achieve enosis by diplomacy, but extremists implemented a terror campaign against British and

FACTS AND FIGURES

Official names: *Kipriaki Dimokratia (Greek) and Kibris Cumhuriyeti (Turkish) (Republic of Cyprus)*

Status: *Independent state*

Capital: *Nicosia*

Major towns: *Limassol, Larnaca, Famagusta*

Area: *3,572 square miles (9,251 square kilometers)*

Population: *900,000*

Population density: *252 per square mile (97 per square kilometer)*

Peoples: *78 percent Greeks; 18 percent Turks; 2 percent Armenians; 2 percent others*

Official languages: *Greek and Turkish*

Currencies: *Cypriot pound and Turkish lira*

National days: *Greek Independence Day (March 25); Greek Cypriot National Day (April 1); Cyprus Independence Day (October 1, or November 15 in Turkish area); Ochi Day (October 28)*

Country's name: *The name Cyprus is from the Greek Kypros, meaning "copper," and refers to the island's ancient copper mines.*

Time line:	Stone Age farmers live on Cyprus	Mycenaean Greeks divide Cyprus into city-states	Cyprus becomes part of Byzantine Empire	Cyprus taken over by English	Cyprus taken over by Venetians
	ca. 6000 B.C.E.	1200 B.C.E.	395 C.E.	1191	1489

Cypriot opponents. In response, Turkish Cypriots, who had always opposed enosis, countered it with *taksim* (tahk-SEEM), a desire for partition of the island. In 1960 the United Kingdom gave Cyprus independence, hoping this compromise would end nationalist violence.

The conflict between the Greek-Cypriot majority and the Turkish-Cypriot minority grew so violent that the United Nations sent in troops in 1964. The Turks fled into Nicosia (nih-kuh-SEE-uh) and other enclaves. Matters came to a head in 1974, when troops from mainland Turkey invaded and took over the northern part of the island. About 180,000 Greek Cypriots fled to the south, while 100,000 Turkish Cypriots moved to the safety of the north. Turkish Cypriots separated this area from the rest of Cyprus and declared independence in 1983 as the Turkish Republic of Northern Cyprus.

Turkey is the only country to recognize this state. Today the two regions have their own governments. The buffer zone between them is patroled by United Nations, Greek Cypriot, and Turkish Cypriot troops, and soldiers from mainland Greece and Turkey.

The People of Cyprus

Modern Cyprus is a divided nation, split between the Greek-Cypriot majority and the Turkish-Cypriot minority. As a rule, each group keeps to its part of the island. The religious split directly reflects the ethnic split, with the Greek Cypriots in the south belonging to the Eastern Orthodox Christian Church and the Turkish Cypriots in the north following Islam. There are also Roman Catholics, Christian Maronites (who hold a mixture of Orthodox and Catholic beliefs), and Jews.

Most Turkish Cypriots follow the Sunni branch of Islam, but they are not as strict as Muslims in Turkey. Some drink alcohol, and more of the women wear Western-style dress.

Northern Cyprus observes traditional Islamic holidays.

A parade in Paphos (PAH-fas) to mark Ochi (OE-hee) Day. In addition to their own special days, Greek Cypriots celebrate all the Greek public holidays.

Cyprus ruled by Ottoman Turks	Cyprus ruled by British	Independence	Turkish invasion and partition of Cyprus	Turkish Republic of Northern Cyprus declares its independence
1571–1878	**1878–1960**	**1960**	**1974**	**1983**

The most important is Ramadan (RAH-muh-dahn), held in the ninth month of the lunar year. During the daylight hours of Ramadan, healthy adult Muslims do not eat or drink. The month ends with the festival of Eid al-Fitr (ID uhl-FIT-reh: Ending the Fast). Cypriot Muslims exchange gifts and enjoy a feast that includes charcoal-grilled lamb.

Christian Celebrations

For Cypriot Christians, the key celebrations are Easter and the period over Christmas, New Year, and Epiphany.

On Easter Saturday night, people burn effigies of Judas, the disciple who betrayed Jesus, on a bonfire called a lampradjia *(lahm-pra-JEE-ah). Everyone leaves midnight mass holding candles and goes home to eat* avgolemono *(ahv-goe-LEH-moe-noe: egg and lemon rice soup). On Easter Sunday the main meal is clay-baked lamb, to remind people that Jesus is the Lamb of God.*

Children believe Saint Basil visits with presents on December 31. On New Year's Day people exchange presents and share a cake called a vasilopitta *(vah-see-LOE-pee-tah). A coin is hidden somewhere in the cake. There is a slice for everyone, and also one for Jesus Christ and one for the house. Finding the coin brings good luck.*

At Epiphany (January 6) there is a special ritual in the seaside villages. After mass the priest leads a procession down to the sea and throws in his crucifix. Young men dive in and rescue it. Doves are set free, and local boats sound their horns.

A family enjoys a wedding reception in Turkish Cyprus. Cypriot Muslims follow a relaxed code of dress. While many older women cover their heads, most younger ones do not.

Daily Life in Town and Country

The island is a popular tourist destination, and many townspeople work in hotels and restaurants or at historic sites. There are also jobs in the oil refineries and in factories that produce cement, bricks, and mosaic tiles. Other industries include the production of cigarettes, shoes, clothes, and beer. Some people work in quarries and mines, extracting the country's natural resources of limestone, asbestos, chromite, iron pyrites, gypsum, and marble.

Away from the towns there are family-owned farms and vineyards. The hot climate suits citrus fruits and grapes. Potatoes, grains, and tobacco grow too. The citrus groves are mainly found in the Turkish part of the island, around Morphou (MAWR-foo). Farmers working on the dry central plains have to irrigate their land. Many farmers keep livestock, especially

These young Greek Cypriots are surfing the Internet in a cybercafé in the southwestern city of Paphos. All Cyprus's main cities have Internet cafés.

academic or work-related studies such as tourism. In Turkish Cyprus there are no state-run nurseries. Children go to elementary school from age six to fifteen, then to high school until they are eighteen.

Dips and Stews

When Cypriots eat out, they usually order *meze* (meh-ZEH), a succession of around twenty starter-sized dishes. Meze includes dips such as hummus (chickpea paste) and *tzatzíki* (tzah-TZEE-kee: yogurt, cucumber, and mint), salads, *halloumi* (ha-LOOM-ee: a cheese made of sheep's and goat's milk, usually flavored with mint) fried in filo pastry, stuffed vine leaves, and lots of other appetizers, many of which are mopped up with unleavened sesame bread. At home, stews are popular: *stifado* (stee-FAH-thoe) is chunks of beef or hare cooked in onion, wine, vinegar, and spices; *tava* (tah-VAH) is made with lamb, tomato, and onions. Other lamb dishes include *kleftico* (KLEF-

sheep. Along the coast, fishing provides a more profitable way of life than farming.

Most Cypriots live in apartment buildings. There is a serious housing problem. After the Turkish invasion, Greek Cypriots in the occupied part lost their homes. Since then, the government of Greek Cyprus has built housing estates that are free for the poorest Cypriots. There are also lots of self-built homes on land provided by the government.

Health care is free for all in Turkish Cyprus, and in Greek Cyprus for people on low incomes or with large families. Cyprus has over a dozen hospitals and more are being built. There are also more than one hundred private clinics. Demand for health care is rising as people live longer. On average, Cypriot men live to 74 and women to 79 years of age.

In Greek Cyprus children attend nursery school from age three to five, then elementary school until they are eleven. High school is split into three years of *gymnasium* (gim-NAH-see-oem), covering general subjects, then three years of *lyceum* (LEE-kee-oem), which can be either

Cleaning octopus leaves this fisher's hands black with the ink they produce. Octopus may be grilled fresh from the sea or hung up to dry in the sunshine and used later in stews.

tee-koe), lamb baked in an outdoor clay oven; moussaka (moo-sah-KAH), a meat dish with eggplant; and *kontosouvli* (kon-doe-SOO-vlee), lamb kebabs cooked on a rod. Fish and prawns are grilled on a barbecue and served with a squeeze of lemon and a splash of olive oil.

Dessert is usually fresh fruit, such as oranges, melons, or grapes. Cypriots also love sticky, honey-sweetened pastries. They eat these with strong, thick Turkish-style coffee, served in tiny cups. Cypriot wine has been made for thousands of years. The country also produces strong brandies, called *raki* (rah-KEE) in Turkish and *zivania* (zee-VAH-nee-ah) in Greek.

Cypriot Culture and Art

Cypriot entertainments include folk music and dance. Music is often provided by a stringed instrument called the *bouzouki* (boo-ZOO-kee). The *kalamatianos* (kah-lah-mah-tee-ah-NOES) dance originated in Kalamata, Greece, and is performed all over Cyprus. The men and women stand in a row with their hands on each other's shoulders.

This nun is an icon painter. Icons are formal portraits of Christ and the saints. They are held in great reverence by Orthodox Christians (see GREECE).

Almost every Cypriot village celebrates its own festival or fair during July or August. It is a time for friends and families to get together. Folk dancers and musicians perform, and farmers display their best produce. There are also displays of flowers and local art. Craftspeople show off their wares. Street sellers offer *lokmades* (lok-MAH-thez), or deep-fried pastry balls soaked in thin honey, and there are sports, games, and dances.

The Cypriots are famous for their folk crafts, notably lace, wickerwork, and pottery. Jars called *pithari* (pee-THAH-ree) are made from terra-cotta, and left out in the sun to bake dry.

Theater has also been enjoyed in Cyprus since ancient Greek times. The state-run Cyprus Theatre Organization puts on eight productions each year. In the Turkish north, shadow puppet shows, called *karagöz* (kah-rah-GYOEZ), have been popular for more than four hundred years.

Lefkara Lace

The village of Pano Lefkara (PAH-noe luhf-KAH-ruh), at the base of the Troodos (TROO-does) Mountains, has been famous for its fine handmade lace since the Middle Ages. Most of the craftspeople are women. They sit in their doorways making intricate tablecloths and invite passersby to see their lace. These days the main buyers are tourists, but legend has it that Leonardo da Vinci, the famous artist and scientist, took some lace back to Italy as a souvenir in the 1500s.

CZECH REPUBLIC

THE CZECH REPUBLIC IS A MOUNTAINOUS LANDLOCKED COUNTRY in central Europe.

The southwest of the country contains many lakes. In the east, just north of the city of Brno, is a limestone region that contains many caves and underground lakes and rivers.

Mountain ranges run along most of the country's borders. The highest peak, Mount Sněžka, rises to 5,255 feet (1,602 meters) in the Krkonoše Mountains, along the border with Poland. Between the mountain ranges lie forests, farmland, and rivers. About one-third of the country is forested.

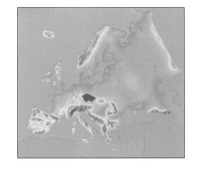

CLIMATE

The Czech Republic has warm summers and cold winters. There is a lot of snow in the winter months, especially in the mountains.

	Prague
Average January temperature:	*30°F (−1°C)*
Average July temperature:	*66°F (19°C)*
Average annual precipitation:	*16 in. (41 cm)*

A picture of rural life in the Czech Republic today. A family travels home in their horse-drawn cart with the young boy's bicycle on the back.

90

Celtic and Slavic Settlements

The region of today's Czech (CHEHK) Republic has been inhabited for at least 25,000 years. However, the remains of the first fortified settlements are known to have been the work of Celtic peoples in the 200s and 100s B.C.E. One Celtic tribe, the Boii (BOE-yih), probably gave their name to Bohemia. The Celts (KEHLTS) were conquered by Germanic tribes in the 300s C.E. They in turn were displaced by invasions of Slavic people coming from the east. Some Slavs (SLAHVZ) united in the 800s to form the Great Moravian (muh-RAE-vee-uhn) Empire. These Slavic people converted to Christianity in 863.

The Great Moravian Empire was destroyed by the Magyars (Hungarians) in the early 900s. In the same century the state of Bohemia (boe-HEE-mee-uh) was created. It centered around Prague (PRAHG) and included some lands of the former Moravian Empire. By the twelfth century a kingdom had emerged that was recognizable as Czech and composed for the most part of Slavic people. The Slavs were joined during the thirteenth century by German townspeople and farmers, who were invited to settle in Prague and other major cities and along Bohemia's western frontier.

The Golden Age of Bohemia

Bohemia's golden age came under King Charles IV, who came to the throne in 1347. Charles IV made Prague one of the most important cities in Europe. He founded the first university in central Europe there in 1348 and attracted to his court some of the best architects, artists, and thinkers of the day. Under Charles IV, the Czech language was favored over Latin (the language used in the courts of Europe) and German. Priests began to write religious stories and chronicles in the Czech language.

In the early 1400s a Czech priest called Jan Hus and his followers, the Hussites,

FACTS AND FIGURES

Official name: Česká Republika (Czech Republic)

Status: Independent state

Capital: Prague

Major towns: Brno, Ostrava, Plzeň, Olomouc, Liberec

Area: 30,450 square miles (78,866 square kilometers)

Population: 10,300,000

Population density: 338 per square mile (131 per square kilometer)

Peoples: 94 percent Czechs; 4 percent Slovaks; 2 percent Poles, Germans, Jews, and Roma

Official language: Czech

Currency: Koruna

National days: Liberation Day (May 8); Death of Jan Hus (July 6); Foundation of Czechoslovakia (October 28)

Country's name: The country is named after the Czechs, the Slavic people who settled in the region more than twelve hundred years ago.

Time line:	Celts build fortified settlements	Germanic tribes conquer Celts	Great Moravian Empire founded	Magyars destroy Great Moravian Empire; state of Bohemia created
	ca. 200s B.C.E.	300s C.E.	800s	900s

PRAGA
Regni Bohemiæ metropolis

A view of Prague from around 1600. At this time Prague and the kingdom of Bohemia were under the rule of the Austrian monarchs, the Hapsburgs.

accused the Catholic Church of Rome of corruption in many aspects of religious life. Hus was eventually burned at the stake, but many Czechs identified with him. As a consequence, Bohemia experienced fifteen years of warfare when neighboring Catholic countries invaded Bohemia to eradicate Hussite ideas.

Austrian Domination

Bohemia came under the rule of a powerful Austrian family, the Hapsburgs, in 1526. The Hapsburgs were Roman Catholics who controlled vast areas of western and central Europe. During the rest of the 1500s, Europe became divided between countries faithful to the Roman Catholic church and those adopting the new Protestant religions

(see GERMANY). The continent was plunged into the Thirty Years' War in 1618. This conflict started in Prague, where a revolt against Hapsburg rule by the Hussites was crushed. Many Czechs were killed, and towns and villages were destroyed. Protestantism was banned, and for a long time, the Czechs were kept firmly under the control of the Hapsburg family.

Many struggles against the rule of the Hapsburgs took place in the early 1800s. In 1848 people across Europe rose up against the old aristocratic types of government. Czechs fought to give Bohemia its own constitution and a greater degree of self-government, but they were defeated.

During the nineteenth century, Czechs became more and more aware of their close linguistic and cultural links to the neighboring Slovak people who were ruled by Hungary. When the Hapsburgs' Austro-Hungarian Empire was dismantled after its

Charles IV king of Bohemia	Catholic nations invade Bohemia to crush Hussites	Bohemia comes under Hapsburg control	Thirty Years' War; defeat of Protestantism	Revolution by Czechs put down	Czechs and Slovaks united in Czechoslovakia
1347–1378	1419–1434	1526	1618–1648	1848	1918

defeat in World War I (1914–1918), the new nation of Czechoslovakia (cheh-koe-sloe-VAH-kee-uh) was created, combining the Czech people with the Slovaks to the east.

War and Communism

In 1939 the Germans, under Adolf Hitler, invaded Austria and then turned on Czechoslovakia, where about three million Germans lived. Czechoslovakia was wealthy in terms of coal and other minerals useful for industrial and military purposes. Hitler took it all. Very soon afterward, the world was at war. In 1944 and 1945 western Bohemia was liberated by U.S. troops and the rest of the country by soldiers of the communist Soviet Union. Three million Germans were deported.

The strong Czechoslovak Communist Party, supported by the Soviet Union, took control of the police and army. In 1948 the Communist Party organized a successful coup and the formation of a communist-led government. The communists held power until 1989. Industries and agriculture were nationalized, and all opposition was suppressed. Many opponents of the government were put in prison or labor camps, and some were executed. In the 1960s there was a minor loosening of the stranglehold that government had over the people's lives. In 1968 political censorship was abolished, and a reform movement, later known as the "Prague Spring," grew. The Soviet Union and its allies sent in more than 200,000 soldiers to reimpose their authority. After this, government returned to hard-line tactics to keep the people under control. Nonetheless, the Prague Spring had started something that through the 1970s and 1980s was to grow into an irresistible demand for democracy and freedom.

Students protest the invasion of their country by Soviet troops in 1968. The soldiers were sent to suppress the Czechoslovak reform movement known as the Prague Spring.

Germany invades	Country liberated by U.S. and Soviet troops	Coup leads to communist-led government	Industry and agriculture nationalized; many people put in prison or labor camps	Soviet troops invade to end reforms	Charter 77 formed
1939	1944–1945	1948	1950s	1968	1977

Charter 77

In 1977 a Czech punk rock band called The Plastic People of the Universe *was arrested by the communist government for "crimes against the state." Out of the protests that followed, a group called* Charter 77 *was formed to monitor human rights abuses. Charter 77 was mainly made up of dissidents living in Prague. Throughout the 1980s, Charter 77 provided a focus for people around the country who wanted to end the decades of communist rule. However, its members had to be very careful in what they did and said, because imprisonment was the penalty for being too openly critical of the Communist Party. The most famous member of Charter 77 was Václav Havel, the man who eventually led the country out of the years of communist dictatorship.*

from power in a revolution that did not cost any lives. The writer, and member of the human rights group Charter 77, Václav Havel was made president. In 1993, after peaceful negotiations, Czechoslovakia was divided into two independent republics, the Czech Republic and Slovakia.

The Czech Republic now looks to western European countries and to the United States for support. A good industrial base and a very healthy tourist industry are helping the country to grow and develop. Reforms have given the people greater freedom and power over their own affairs. The country became a member of the North Atlantic Treaty Organization (NATO) in 1999, and the government has applied to join the European Union as well. Successes in soccer and ice hockey and at the Olympics in the 1990s have encouraged national pride as the Czech Republic moves toward finding its place in the twenty-first century.

The Velvet Revolution

Mass protests and demonstrations in 1989, when the rest of the communist bloc was undergoing similar upheaval, finally led to what has been called the Velvet Revolution. In November of that year, the communists were removed

This woman is celebrating the Velvet Revolution that took place in 1989. She is holding up a photograph of Václav Havel, who became president of the post-communist country.

Protests against communist government	Free elections; Václav Havel president	Czechoslovakia splits into Czech Republic and Slovakia	Czech Republic applies to join European Union	Czech Republic joins NATO
1989	**1990**	**1993**	**1996**	**1999**

A Roma band plays violins and an accordion at a celebration. The Roma people of the region still face abuse, and they are sometimes the victims of violence in the Czech Republic.

The People of the Czech Republic

By far the majority of people living in the Czech Republic are Czech by ethnic origin. The second biggest ethnic group is the Slovaks. There are around 115,000 Roma (ROE-muh) people, and there are very small numbers of Poles, Germans, and Jews.

The Roma have always been a wandering folk, disliking the settled way of life of most of the people around them. Many moved from Slovakia to the Czech Republic after 1993, causing an upsurge of anti-Roma sentiment. Graffiti with sentiments against the Roma has appeared on walls in Prague, and a poll showed that well over half the Czech population thinks that the Roma are dirty and criminal. Many Roma have left the Czech Republic, hoping to find a better life in western Europe.

Today, about 40 percent of people are Roman Catholic, with the Protestant faith represented by a smaller minority. There is

Let's Talk Czech

The Czech language has developed from the language of the early Slavic settlers. It is very similar to the language of the Czechs' neighbors, the Slovaks.

děkuju (DEH-kuh-yuh)	*thank you*
ahoj (A-hoy)	*hello*
prosím (PRAH-siem)	*please*
dobré ráno (DAHB-ree RAE-nah)	*good morning*
dobrý večer (DAHB-rie VEH-chehr)	*good evening*
Jak se máte? (YAK SEH MAE-teh)	*How are you?*

Ve svěžím a čerstvém rytmu

SUPERMARKETY DELVITA

A supermarket slogan gives an example of the Czech language. In Czech the stress is almost always on the first syllable of a word.

A peasant couple harvest their crop in the shadow of the Dukovany nuclear power plant, near Třebíč (tuhr-ZEH-beech). This plant has been responsible for the high levels of radioactivity in the area.

a great deal of respect for different beliefs throughout the country. However, active worship in churches, as in so many other European countries, is very low.

Industry and the Environment

The Czech Republic has one of the strongest economies in eastern Europe. The region was industrialized early in the nineteenth century. By the 1930s it was second only to Germany in industrial output and listed as one of the top ten most developed states in the world. A poor quality coal called lignite was mined, which provided the fuel for this industrial growth. However, this source of energy has left one of the most polluted atmospheres in Europe.

In winter, smogs are a big problem in the cities. Cold air traps poisonous gases, including sulfur dioxide. Acid rain, formed when these gases mix with rain in the air, has destroyed huge areas of forest, especially in northern Bohemia. Since the collapse of communism, the government has tried to clean up industry, mainly by switching from coal as the principal energy source for industry to gas, which is cleaner.

The economy of the Czech Republic still relies on heavy industry. The country produces steel, machinery, cars, weapons, plastics, glass,

Czech glassware is famous all over the world for its high quality and delicacy. These workers in a glass factory are attaching a red-hot glass handle to a jug.

shoes, cement, and beer. In 1991 the German car manufacturer Volkswagen teamed up with Skoda, the Czech company, a move that widened the market for Skoda cars.

The economy is reviving once again since the upheavals of 1989, helped by the enormous growth in tourism. Millions of people visit the Czech Republic every year, spending billions of dollars in the country.

The majority of the working population have a job, and there is a healthy export market to both former communist allies, such as Russia, and to western Europe.

Many countries invested money in the Czech Republic and its industries during the 1990s. At the top of this list is Germany, with the United States, France, and Austria following. The fact that these countries have put millions of dollars into the Czech Republic is seen as a measure of confidence in the country's future.

A famous landmark in Prague is the Charles Bridge (seen here), built in 1357. It is lined with statues and was the only bridge across the Vltava River until the 1800s.

Historic Prague

Prague is one of the most beautiful cities in the world. Its history is evident in the many old and magnificent buildings and statues. Under Bohemia's greatest ruler, Charles IV, Prague became a university city. Further building took place in the 1700s under the Hapsburgs. Prague today is a UNESCO (United Nations Educational, Scientific, and Cultural Organization) World Heritage site.

Prague is split in two by the Vltava (VUHL-tuh-vuh) River. Seventeen bridges link the two halves. Nestled in a fertile valley, the city is surrounded by hills topped by castles. One of the oldest parts of the city is Hradčany (RAHD-kuh-nee), with a royal medieval castle, some fine churches, and museums. Malá Strana (MAHL-uh STRAH-nuh: the Little Quarter) and Staré Město (XXX STAH-rae MAES-toe: Old Town) are very distinct areas, almost like little cities within the larger city.

Life in the Czech Republic Today

The Czech Republic has moved quickly to a capitalist economy, in which the government does not interfere. Times have been hard for the big traditional industries, such as steel manufacturing and coal mining. Large towns and cities such as Prague and Brno (BUHR-naw), the second largest city, have seen the fastest rate of change. Here, a skilled and educated workforce has adapted to new jobs and ways of working. Although salaries are still low compared to western Europe and the United States, they compare well with other former communist countries. Country towns and villages tend to lag behind in terms of development.

Brno (the largest city in the eastern region of Moravia) was industrialized in the nineteenth century, becoming a textile manufacturing and engineering city. It grew rapidly in the 1960s and 1970s, when the communists built ugly, high-rise

Plzeň is an industrial city with a population of more than 150,000. It is home to the world-famous Pilsner beer and has a museum of Czech brewing.

Taking the Waters

Karlovy Vary (KAHR-law-vee VAHR-ee) is a spa town in the far west of the Czech Republic. There are twelve springs in the town. The water is hot, coming out of the ground at between 104°F (40°C) and 158°F (70°C). It can shoot almost 40 feet (12 meters) into the air. Legend says that the waters were found by King Charles IV's dog, which fell in and was boiled alive. Charles IV founded the town in 1358, and over the centuries many famous people have visited, seeking a cure from the mineral-rich waters or a rest. These include Emperor Peter the Great of Russia; the writers Leo Tolstoy, Karl Marx, and J. W. von Goethe; and the first man in space, Yuri Gagarin.

apartment buildings called *paneláky* (PA-neh-lae-kih) for the workers. They were constructed quickly of low-cost materials and now need continual repairs. Many of these homes are cramped, and living rooms will often double as bedrooms.

Country people mainly work on the land, cultivating wheat, oats, rye, oilseed rape, peas, beets, and corn, and keeping a few chickens and geese.

During the 1990s the government set about tackling major causes of early death among Czech people. These include heart disease and pollution-related illnesses (such as lung disease). The average life expectancy for a man is 71 years and for a woman 78 years.

All Czech children have to attend school between the ages of six and fifteen. Parents can choose from state-controlled, private, or religious schools for their children. The majority attend the state-controlled elementary school, called *základní škola* (ZAE-klad-nie SHKAH-la). Most villages still have these elementary schools, but pupils wanting to further their education must sometimes travel to the larger towns to attend high schools. The larger cities, such as Prague and Brno, have universities and colleges.

Dumplings, Cakes, and Beer

Czech food is generally very nourishing and filling. It shows a mix of Austrian and Hungarian influences, as well as bringing something special of its own to the table. A typical meal might include a starter of smoked Prague ham, called *Pražká šunka* (PRAHZ-skae SHUN-ka), followed by *drštkova polévka* (DOORSHT-kae-vae PAH-leev-ka: tripe soup). The main course could be either hot or cold. It consists mainly of meat, though some fish is eaten occasionally. A favorite dish is meat with flat dumplings, called *knedlíky* (NEED-lie-kih). Desserts are equally hearty. Dishes such as coffee cake, plum jam cake, and pancakes are very popular. One real Czech specialty is dumplings filled with fresh fruit.

The Czechs are very proud of their beer brewing traditions. The original Budweiser beer, Budvar, comes from the Czech Republic. So too does Pilsner, a world-famous beer from Plzeň. Wine is produced in southern Moravia. Among stronger drinks,

Czech children have fun playing games in a wooden drum. These children enjoy a good education system, and sports are encouraged.

becherovka (BEH-keh-rahv-ka), a herb liquor from Karlovy Vary, is supposed to be good for the health.

Czech Literature

The Czechs have produced some world-class writers. In the nineteenth century, when Czech nationalism emphasized the importance of the Czech language, writers such as Alois Jirásek (1851–1930) rallied to the call. Jirásek wrote many novels about the history of his country.

Franz Kafka (1883–1924), born in Prague, chose to write in German. His works include *The Trial, The Castle,* and *The Metamorphosis.* He wrote about nightmarish

worlds in which individuals are totally unable to control their lives. His dark portrayals of life were to come true for many under the communist government.

Milan Kundera (born in Brno in 1929) is another internationally acclaimed Czech writer. He left the country in 1975. Many of his books, such as *The Joke* and *The Book of*

Christmas Customs

Czechs take their Christmas celebrations very seriously. These begin on December 4, the feast day of Saint Barbara. People buy cherry tree branches, which they hope will bloom by Christmas. On December 5, groups of three people, dressed as an angel, the devil, and Saint Nicholas, walk the streets. Good children receive fruit and candy from the angel, but children who have been bad are offered lumps of coal or potatoes by the devil. Saint Nicholas, the patron saint of Christmas, has a white beard, a long robe, and a bishop's hat.

At Christmas time Czech families traditionally eat carp, a sort of fish. Carp are sold live from large barrels in the streets. On Christmas Eve religious people do not eat anything until the evening, when the first star appears in the sky. Then the feast can begin, followed by presents for the children of the family.

Children dressed as Saint Nicholas (in the bishop's hat with a cross on it) and the devil. On December 5 they walk the streets as part of the traditional Saint Nicholas celebrations.

Puppet Theater

For hundreds of years Czechs of all ages have enjoyed puppet shows. Today there are more than fifteen permanent puppet theaters in the country. In Prague are wonderful shops that sell all kinds of puppets. Some of the country's best-known theaters are also in Prague, including the National Marionette Theater, the Magic Lantern Theater, and Puppet Kingdom.

Laughter and Forgetting, deal with Czech events and the lives of the people. Kundera made fun of the communists; in return, the government took away his Czech citizenship and banned some of his works.

Team Sports and Tennis Stars

The people of the Czech Republic are great sports enthusiasts. The most popular sports are soccer, ice hockey, volleyball, tennis, and kickball. The last sport is a Czech invention, similar to volleyball, but the players use their feet rather than their hands to push the ball over a low net.

Czechoslovakia's soccer team came second in the 1934 and 1962 World Cups

Outdoor sports are very popular in the Czech Republic. These canoeists are learning to paddle through fast-flowing water under the watchful eye of an instructor.

and were European champions in 1976. After the breakup of Czechoslovakia, the Czech Republic's team came second in the European championships of 1996. Czechoslovakia's national ice hockey team was for many years ranked in the top five teams in the world, and the Czech Republic's team won the 1998 Olympic ice hockey title.

Another popular sport in the Czech Republic is tennis. Martina Navratilova stands out as one of the greatest players of all time, and Ivan Lendl, Jana Novotna, Helena Sukova, and Hana Mandlikova have all won international fame.

Children have plenty of leisure time to enjoy these popular sports. Skiing is taught at school. Summer camps for children introduce them to such sports as rock climbing and canoeing. Walking and camping are also popular. Families often get away on weekends to country houses called *chata* (KAH-ta).

A fashionable bar and restaurant in Prague. Czech people are very sociable and like to go out to meet friends for a drink or a meal.

Music and Nationalism

Three great Czech composers, Bedřich Smetana (1824–1884), Antonín Dvořák (1841–1904), and Leoš Janáček (1854–1928), were nationalists who drew on folk music for their themes and melodies.

Smetana wrote operas on Czech themes to encourage nationalist feeling. He used the most famous Czech dance, the polka, in his opera The Bartered Bride.

Dvořák's roots were in the peasant culture of Bohemia. To earn money while studying music in Prague, he played folk tunes on the viola in cafés. All the great instrumental music he later composed shows its debt to folk culture.

Janáček was born in Moravia and worked all his life in Brno. He was an expert on Moravian folk music, but he is best known for his operas, in which the vocal lines copy the rhythms of Czech speech.

Two elderly women from southern Moravia wear traditional clothes at a local festival. Their dresses are decorated with intricate lacework, and they wear patterned headscarves.

Music and Festivals

The Czech Republic is today a very lively place to live. Newer types of entertainment—rock music, jazz, movies from around the world, and nightclubs—are combined with the classical pleasures of ballet, opera, music, theater, and art galleries. During the summer months classical music is played outdoors. Prague is the center of much of this activity.

Jazz is very popular with the people of Prague. There are many clubs and bars all over the city that specialize in jazz music.

The Czech Republic's folk music and dance traditions are celebrated with festivals throughout the year and in every part of the country. One of the most popular is the festival held at Domažlice (doe-muhz-LEE-chuh), where folk songs, traditional dances, and bagpipe music from south and west Bohemia are performed. An international folk festival is held every June at Strážnice (STRAHZ-nih-chuh) in Moravia. In this region local bands still play at weddings, dances, and other celebrations. Here, cimbalom bands are popular. The cimbalom is a box-shaped instrument whose strings are struck with small hammers. In Moravia it is one of the instruments in a band that includes fiddles, clarinets, and string bass.

A folk band from southern Bohemia play fiddles, string bass, and bagpipes. Bagpipes are very popular in southern and western Bohemia.

103

Glossary

acid rain: rainfall containing chemical pollutants. It is produced when fossil fuels are burned. Their by-products react with water and sunlight in the atmosphere to create weak acids. When they fall to Earth as rain, they damage trees, soils, and waterways.

annexed: describes a region taken over by another.

aristocratic: belonging to the nobility, an elite or privileged group within society.

Byzantine Empire: an empire in the eastern Mediterranean region, based in Constantinople (Istanbul) from 474 to 1453 C.E.

capitalist: describes an economic system in which land, factories, and other ways of producing goods are owned and controlled by individuals, not the government.

cease-fire: a military order to stop fighting.

cede: to grant or give up.

censor: to limit free expression or communication.

center-left: supporting moderate socialist political policies. Socialism is a political theory in which the community as a whole controls land, property, industry, and money and organizes them for the good of all the people.

coalition: a temporary alliance between or among political parties or groups of people.

communist: describes a theory that suggests that all property belongs to the community and that work should be organized for the common good.

cosmopolitan: multicultural or multiracial; open to international influences.

democracy: a state ruled by the people, in which government is carried out by representatives elected by the public.

dialect: a nonstandard version of a language, as spoken in a particular region or by a particular group of people.

diplomacy: the official dealings between or among the governments of two or more nations or peoples, each represented by their appointed representative (usually an ambassador).

dissident: a person who disagrees with his or her government or its policies.

duchy: a state ruled by a duke or duchess.

European Union: an alliance of European nations committed to economic union and closer political integration.

genocide: the planned killing of a whole people or ethnic group.

guerrilla: a member of an irregular fighting force whose tactics include ambushes, surprise attacks, and sabotage rather than intense, close battles with the enemy.

humanitarian: describes an action or policy that aims to help people and relieve suffering.

hydroelectric: of or related to production of electricity from waterpower. The force of a waterfall or dammed river may be used to produce electricity in a power station.

linguistic: pertaining to language.

medieval: of or pertaining to the Middle Ages (the years from ca. 500 to ca. 1500 C.E.).

militia: a group of ordinary citizens organized for military service; they are not a part of a regular army.

nationalize: to make something the property of the nation or state.

NATO: the North Atlantic Treaty Organization; a group of countries (includes the United States, Canada, many European states, and Turkey) who agree by treaty to give each other military help.

Nazi: pertaining to the National Socialist German Worker's Party, which controlled the government of Germany from 1933 to 1945 under Adolf Hitler.

Ottoman Empire: an Islamic empire, founded in 1299, which finally collapsed in 1922. At its peak, from the fifteenth to the seventeenth centuries, it controlled Asia Minor, the eastern Mediterranean region, and large parts of southeastern Europe. From 1453 its capital was Constantinople (now Istanbul), in Turkey.

pharmaceuticals: medical drugs.

radioactivity: the property possessed by some elements or isotopes of spontaneously emitting radiation in a nuclear reaction. Radioactivity is harmful to living things.

referendum: a vote on important or controversial matters.

republic: a country in which power rests with the people and their elected representatives.

sanctions: measures taken to prevent or limit trade with a particular country. The aim is to force that country to change its political system or its policies.

Soviet Union (Union of Soviet Socialist Republics): a federation of fifteen communist republics in eastern Europe and Asia created in 1922 and dissolved in 1991.

subsidized: provided with money by a government to keep the price of goods low.

Sunni: a group comprising about four out of every five Muslims. Sunni Muslims aim to follow the Sunnah (the example of prayer and good behavior set by the Prophet Muhammad) in their daily lives.

tripe: the stomach tissue of a ruminant, usually an ox, used as food.

United Nations: an alliance, founded in 1945, that today includes most of the countries in the world. Its aim is to encourage international cooperation and peace.

World War I: a conflict that broke out in Europe in 1914. The Entente powers, or Allies, (which included the United Kingdom, France, and Russia) fought the Central Powers (which included Austria-Hungary, Germany, and Turkey). The United States joined the Allies in 1917. The war ended in 1918.

World War II: a war that began in Europe in 1939 and spread to involve many other countries worldwide. It ended in 1945. The United Kingdom, France, the Soviet Union, the United States, Canada, Australia, New Zealand, and other European countries fought against Germany, Italy, and Japan.

Further Reading

Internet Sites

Look under Countries A to Z in the Atlapedia Online Web Site at
    http://www.atlapedia.com
Look under Country Listing in the CIA World Factbook Web Site at
    http://www.odci.gov/cia/publications/factbook
Use the Country Locator Maps in the World Atlas Web Site at
    http://www.worldatlas.com/aatlas/world.htm
Look under the alphabetical country listing using the Infoplease Atlas at
    http://www.infoplease.com/countries.html
Look under World Countries in the World Encyclopedia Web Site at
    http://www.emulateme.com
Look under the alphabetical country listing in the Yahooligans Around the World Directory at
    http://www.yahooligans.com/around_the_world/countries

Bosnia and Herzegovina

Flint, David. *Bosnia: Can There Ever Be Peace? (Topics in the News)*. Austin, TX: Raintree/Steck Vaughn, 1995.
Isaac, John (Photographer), Keith Elliot Greenberg, Bruce Glassman (Editor). *Bosnia: Civil War in Europe (Children in Crisis)*. Woodbridge, CT: Blackbirch Marketing, 1997.
Ricchiardi, Sherry. *Bosnia: The Struggle for Peace*. Brookfield, CT: Millbrook Press, 1996.
Yancey, Diane. *Life in War-Torn Bosnia (The Way People Live)*. San Diego, CA: Lucent Books, 1996.

Bulgaria

Otfinoski, Steven and Andrew Wentick. *Bulgaria (Nations in Transition)*. New York: Facts on File, Inc., 1998.
Popescu, Julian. *Bulgaria (Major World Nations)*. Philadelphia, Pa.: Chelsea House Publishers, 2000.
Resnick, Abraham. *Bulgaria (Enchantment of the World)*. Chicago, IL: Children's Press, 1995.
Rodgers, Mary M. *Bulgaria in Pictures (Visual Geography Series)*. Minneapolis, MN: Lerner Publications Company, 1994.
Stavreva, Kirilka. *Bulgaria (Cultures of the World)*. Tarrytown, NY: Marshall Cavendish, 1998.

Croatia

Cooper, Robert. *Croatia (Cultures of the World)*. Tarrytown, NY: Marshall Cavendish, 2001.

Cyprus

Cyprus in Pictures (Visual Geography Series). Minneapolis, MN: Lerner Publications Company, 1992.
Spilling, Michael. *Cyprus (Cultures of the World)*. Tarrytown, NY: Marshall Cavendish, 2000.

Czech Republic

Czech Republic in Pictures (Visual Geography Series). Minneapolis, MN: Lerner Publications Company, 1995.
Humphreys, Rob. *Czech Republic (Country Insights, City and Village Life)*. Austin, TX: Raintree/Steck Vaughn, 1998.
Sioras, Efstathia. *Czech Republic (Cultures of the World)*. Tarrytown, NY: Marshall Cavendish, 1999.

Index

Page numbers in *italic* indicate illustrations.

Page numbers in *italic* indicate illustrations.